# WASHINGTON
## MERRY-GO-ROUND

71

R. S. Allen

1931
### HORACE LIVERIGHT, INC.
### NEW YORK

54270

Published, July, 1931
Second printing, July, 1931
Third printing, July, 1931
Fourth printing, July, 1931
Fifth printing, July, 1931
Sixth printing, August, 1931
Seventh printing, August, 1931
Eighth printing, August, 1931
Ninth printing, August, 1931
Tenth printing, August, 1931
Eleventh printing, September, 1931
Twelfth printing, September, 1931
Thirteenth printing, September, 1931
Fourteenth printing, September, 1931
Fifteenth printing, October, 1931
Sixteenth printing, October, 1931
Seventeenth printing, October, 1931
Eighteenth printing, November, 1931
Nineteenth printing, November, 1931
Twentieth printing, December, 1931
Twenty-first printing, December, 1931
Twenty-second printing, January, 1932

TO THOSE WHO STILL REACH
FOR THE BRASS RING

# WASHINGTON
## MERRY-GO-ROUND

# CONTENTS

# CHAPTER ONE

## BOILED BOSOMS

*W*ITH the exception of Peking, no other capital in the world equals Washington for the relentless brilliancy with which the spotlight of public attention is fixed upon the comings and goings, the cocktail parties and the amours of the petty people who run the official and social life of the capital of these United States.

If Nick Longworth came back from Cincinnati unexpectedly one autumn night to find himself locked out of his house on Massachusetts Avenue; should Dolly Curtis Gann stop to adjust a slipping stocking before a crowd of shoppers at Woodward and Lothrop's; or should Mrs. Hoover have a dispute with her secretary, Polly Randolph, over flowers for the White House table, most of the dinners and tea parties of Washington are buzzing over the incident twenty-four hours later.

There are two reasons for this. In the first place, Washington is small, and the group which runs its social and official life is even smaller. In the second place, Washington has only one industry—politics.

London, Berlin, Paris, Rome, Moscow, Vienna—all the other great capitals of the world are also vast industrial and commercial centers in which the pompous preening of society is almost swallowed up. Were the capital of the United States located in New York, much of the material for the merry-go-round of Washington would be non-existent. But the capital is not in New York. Instead, it has been plumped down in a placid agricultural community, surrounded by the remnants of a Southern aristocracy which still prides itself on its hounds, hunters and mint-juleps, and which boasts no industry other than the Bureau of Printing and Engraving plus a few river boats which chug sleepily up the Potomac, bringing oysters, Norfolk honeymooners and split pine logs.

Not only is the sole industry of the capital politics, but this industry is concentrated among a very few. Fifty percent of Washington's half million population is of a race which, except when it gathers to cheer Paul Robeson or its lone congressional champion, Oscar De Priest, is neither interested nor admitted into high society.

Of the remaining quarter million people, most are government clerks and the trades-people who support them, leaving the capital's social life almost exclusively in the hands of those who live in the fashionable northwest. This is an area, which, socially speaking, begins at the White House and stretches out Pennsylvania Avenue and Sixteenth Street toward ancient Georgetown to the west and toward *nouveau riche* Chevy Chase on the north.

Within this orbit, divided into many cliques and schisms, throbs a social life as gay, as superficial and as futile as in any capital of Europe.

Broadly speaking, Washington society can be divided into two classes: Those who want to get their names in the papers and those who want to keep them out.

The Cabinet members, the congressional climbers, the Army and Navy, and the professional pushers are all more or less in the first category, while the Young Set, the intellectuals and the fast-riding, hard-drinking poker players are in the second.

There are in Washington a half dozen middle-aged or aging ladies who absolutely dominate the social stage. Their arrival in the fall and their departure in the spring is the order for the ringing up or down of the curtain for the social season. They put the social lions through their tricks—pull them in and out of the social ring. They crack the whip, and they crack it with all the grimness of the tamer who must inspire fawning obedience or retire from the ring.

Most fawned upon among Washington's social whip-crackers are:

Mrs. Joseph (Juliette) Leiter, big, blonde, and the most domineering whip-cracker of them all. Just after the turn of the century she married Joe Leiter, whose boast is that he was "the largest individual holder of wheat in the history of the grain trade," but who, finding it easier to control wheat than his wife, now leaves his enormous mansion on du Pont Circle entirely to her and to the fabulous parties which she gives in the manner but not the quality of the Vanderbilts.

Mrs. James F. (Laura) Curtis, patron saint of those who play for a thousand-dollar limit. She has swallowed her pride just once. Although she left her husband, only to take him back again, Jimmie has gone to live in New York, from which point of vantage he supplies the cash and watches her crack the whip over her little clique as relentlessly as she once cracked it over him.

Eleanor Medill Patterson, formerly Mrs. Eleanor Schlesinger, formerly Countess Gizycka, formerly Eleanor Medill Patterson, one of the most gifted women in Washington but who has dissipated her gifts, for the most part on trivialities.

Alice Roosevelt Longworth, brilliant if not gifted, who through the prestige of her position and the vitriol of her tongue dominates Washington's ultra-fashionable official group more completely than any other whip-cracker in the capital.

One of the most charming things about Washington is that it is almost never without a social, diplomatic or matrimonial war, and as in all one-industry villages these feuds are waged so earnestly that before they are over they line up on one side or the other almost every one in town. Within less than the past twelve months there have been:

The Edward B. McLean-Prince de Ligne War over an alleged dinner-table prank, as the result of which the Belgian

Ambassador, although later forced to retire, received a personal apology from Secretary of State Stimson, and the publisher of the Washington *Post* got a personal apology from the Philadelphia *Record*.

THE PRADO-POINDEXTER WAR over a servant imported from Lima by the wife of the American Ambassador to Peru, which resulted in Counselor Prado, of the Peruvian Embassy in Washington, resigning his post and taking the servant off with him to London.

THE TOTO MACIA-ITALIAN EMBASSY WAR over the unimportant question of incompatibility, which resulted in the beautiful Senora Macia rising up in all her Canadian wrath, fleeing her house at midnight, and secreting her baby in Baltimore.

THE SIAMESE LIQUOR WAR over the right of a legation to transport beverages from Baltimore, which resulted in the entire Diplomatic Corps rebelling against the capital police, with the exception of the gentle British Ambassador, Sir Esme Howard, who promptly announced he would import no more liquor.

THE SALVADOREAN LEGATION-POLICE WAR over the failure of the latter to prevent hi-jackers from absconding with seventeen cases of liquor, and which caused Don Carlos Leiva, having been severely beaten over the head with a flashlight, to sit up in bed and issue scathing statements about repeated attempts to rob his Legation, against which the police offered no protection.

THE DAISY HARRIMAN-RAY BAKER WAR, between two of the most charming and once friendly Democrats of the capital, which resulted when the former came back from Bermuda to find that the latter had dumped 5,000 tons of dirt from the cellar of his new house in the middle of her front lawn.

None of these, of course, could compare with the Dolly Curtis Gann-Alice Roosevelt Longworth precedence war, a war which stirred Washington to the depths of its sensation-loving soul. Unfortunately, this feud, except when Edward Everett Gann calls up the Washington *Daily News* to complain that he is not a "meek" husband, is in a completely comatose stage. Fortunately, however, its place was taken, just before it breathed its last, by the Patterson-Longworth War.

This was not a new battle. Intimate friends of both Eleanor Patterson and Alice Longworth knew that it had been smoldering ever since their debutante days when they had com-

peted for the most eligible men in town. One of them married
a young Congressman from Cincinnati, and the other Count
Joseph Gizycka, a dashing young Polish cavalryman in
Emperor Franz Ferdinand's army.

Later, Cissie Gizycka came back from Warsaw once again
to cramp Alice's style and in later years to tell a story on
herself—which may or may not be true—about a young noble-
man who sat at Alice's right at dinner one evening. After
dinner Cissie monopolized him in an upstairs library. The
following morning she received a note from her hostess which
read as follows:

"Dear Cissie:
"Upon sweeping up the library this morning, tne maid
found several hair-pins which I thought you might need and
which I am returning.

                                          "ALICE."

To which Cissie says she replied:

"Dear Alice:
"Many thanks for the hair-pins. If you had looked on the
chandelier you might also have sent back my shoes and
chewing gum.
"Love,

                                          "CISSIE."

It was at the Republican National Convention of 1920, held
in Chicago, that the first real breach occurred. Cissie Gizycka
had taken a house for the period of the convention, and had
invited as one of her guests William Edgar Borah, shaggy-
maned and shaggy-browed Senator from Idaho. She was
writing a series of human-interest stories on the convention
for the Hearst papers and devoted one of them to a more than
laudatory sketch of Borah. Her house-guest explained that
this was highly embarrassing and cautioned her against any
repetition of her flattery. A day or two later and with all the
ear-marks of having been inspired by an irate Countess
Gizycka, her brother's newspaper, the Chicago Tribune, pub-

lished a scathing editorial, headed "Borah and Blah." Borah's hostess had no connection with the editorial, but both he and Alice Longworth, even then one of his most intimate friends, thought she had. They never forgave Cissie.

Simultaneous with her marriage to Elmer Schlesinger, five years later, Countess Gizycka shook Washington out of its usual slumber by publishing her first book, "Glass Houses." In it she painted, so deftly that no one could mistake them and so brazenly that every one gasped, her old friend and her arch-enemy, Borah and Alice. This widened the breach beyond all repair.

The climax came after Cissie Schlesinger, widowed, always too active to be idle and too intelligent to be content with the routine of society, became editor-in-chief of Hearst's Washington *Herald*. A few weeks later there appeared tucked away at the bottom of the first page an insignificant looking box which brought the *Herald* more circulation in one week than it had ever gained before in years. The box read:

"INTERESTING BUT NOT TRUE

"The news is that Mrs. Alice Longworth will not only be the confidential advisor to Mrs. Ruth Hanna McCormick, but that she will campaign publicly for her lifelong friend. Interesting but not true.

"Mrs. McCormick takes no advice, political or otherwise, from Mrs. Longworth.

"Mrs. Longworth gives no interviews to the press.

"Mrs. Longworth cannot utter in public.

"Her assistance will, therefore, resolve itself, as usual, into posing for photographs."

Letters of approval and protest followed. Washington beamed. A sequel to the Gann-Longworth War had broken out. Editor Patterson, who by that time had resumed her maiden name, tried it again. The majority of her friends frowned and her enemies raved. But as a circulation-getter it was a wow.

It had only one fault. In order to create a first-class row there must be two parties to a dispute. In this case, however, there was only one. Alice refused to hit back. She continued to grant no interviews, make no speeches. She confined her activities to the thing she has always done best, posing for photographs. There is no fun in punching a deflated punching-bag, and Editor Patterson quit.

Since then she has had to be content with giving pretentious dinner parties for Mrs. William Randolph Hearst, interviewing Al Capone and Dr. Einstein, and pretending to enjoy coarse newspaper revelries at which she tries hard to be one of the gang.

\*

ALICE LONGWORTH is one of those rare women who is really absorbed in politics. There are a large number of Washington ladies who flock to the Hill whenever they hear that Borah is going to blast the World Court, or Millard Tydings, Beau Brummel of the Senate, is scheduled to bait the prohibitionists, but not one of them is a regular and consistent follower of all the important things the Senate does. Alice is the sole exception. She not only attends the outstanding Senate debates and committee hearings, but behind the scenes she pulls the wires, as far as she is able, against such pet hates as the World Court, the League of Nations, and the London Naval Treaty.

The part which Mrs. Longworth plays on Capitol Hill, the prestige which she commands throughout Washington, is, of course, resented by other congressional wives, most of whom lead a dull and pompous existence in the red-plush drawing-rooms of the second class hotels which cluster around the Hill, or attend excessively stodgy teas, the guest lists of which they phone at great length to society editors.

It was natural, therefore, that a large number of these estimable ladies should have sided with Dolly Curtis Gann in the social-precedence war against her much more charming and socially powerful opponent, Alice Longworth. Not that they liked Mrs. Gann more; they merely thought of her as one of their own kind.

What was not natural, however, was that Edward Everett Gann, socially unimportant brother-in-law of the Vice President, and Nicholas Longworth, standing at the peak of social supremacy, both should have aided, abetted, spurred and egged on their respective wives in a controversy which for a time rivaled a back-alley cat fight. Edward Everett Gann has been pictured as an "unassuming man" who practised law, never troubled his head about society and led a quiet, happy life until his strapping, titian-haired wife became the official hostess of her half-brother, the Vice President. Then his wife moved him from a vine-clad home in Cleveland Park to a ten-room suite at the Mayflower Hotel, and Mr. Gann's troubles began.

All this was undoubtedly true. But to assume that Mr. Gann objected to his wife's fight for her social rights is equivalent to assuming that Herbert Hoover objects to an adjournment of Congress. Mr. Gann may be shorter and less prepossessing than his wife, he may sidle into inconspicuous corners of drawing-rooms and speak only when spoken to, but he never flinched at the major social war whirling disturbingly around his head. On the contrary, he loved it. He set his jaws and egged his wife into the fray. He subscribed to clipping bureaus. He read with avidity everything written about his wife. If he did not like it, he complained to editors. Most especially he complained about the adjectives "meek" and "mild" when prefixed to his own name. He became Washington's only rival to Italian Ambassador Martino for complaints to the newspapers.

Speaker Longworth, although more thick-skinned about the press, took the controversy just as seriously. He considered his wife's war his war, a war to uphold the dignity of the Speakership. Furthermore, it was a war on behalf of the American people. The Government of the United States, he pointed out, is vested in the people. The Constitution says so. The people are represented by the House of Representatives. It is the body closest to the people. Over this body presides the Speaker. Therefore, the Speaker should go in to dinner ahead of every one except the President.

Longworth, however, overlooked one fact. He, as Speaker of the House of Representatives, was a tremendously powerful individual. He controlled legislation in the House. He was a busy man. He had other things to do than dine out.

Charlie Curtis, on the other hand, wields no more power as presiding officer of the Senate than that of annoying its members with his gavel, as a gnat annoys a horse. To the Vice President, therefore, is given the compensating distinction of being the Administration's chief diner-out.

Actually this is not much of a compensation. Most of the dinners he is called upon to attend are given by such distinguished dowagers as Mrs. Henry F. Dimock, who wears a plumed hat and rides about in a victoria; Mrs. Clarence Crittendon Calhoun, who claims the Earl of Mar as an ancestor and gives Scotch evenings at which she displays her Tennessee husband in kilts; Mrs. François Berger Moran, who claims to be a lineal descendant of George Washington and goes marketing in ermine; Mrs. Larz Anderson, enthusiastic joiner of all possible patriotic societies; plus other starchy affairs at which the Vice President has to sit beside the wives of the Second Assistant Postmaster General, the Commander of the Army Air Corps or the Chief of the Division of International Conferences.

Smart hostesses do not fawn upon Charlie these days. His half-sister, although amiable, tries to hide her mid-western background but every so often reveals it with such abrupt indiscretions as: "Oh, Charley, come kiss me," accompanied by gestures with plump arms. Then, too, when one invites the Vice President to dinner these days it means inviting a small army, since Mr. Gann also must come along. A shadow seems to darken an otherwise scintillating party whenever the vice-presidential trio heaves into sight, and the result is that those who crack the whip with greatest success look to livelier pastures for their dinner guests.

In the official field, grazing is not so good. Among the Cabinet members, Stimson, because he gets up at five-thirty and because of his wife's health, dines out only when diplomatic decency compels it. Secretary of Agriculture Hyde gives stiff and expansive parties at the Mayflower for which he imports potted palms from the Botanical Gardens, and the tall Secretary of the Interior, Ray Lyman Wilbur, although intellectual and witty, is more ill at ease in smoothing the rough edges off a dinner conversation than when facing a senatorial committee on the Federal Power Commission. Frequently, he does not know his guests' names and behind their backs asks whispered advice from other guests as to who they are.

Of the others, Charles Francis Adams, although as taciturn as his Northampton neighbor; Andrew W. Mellon, who loves Washington society so much he is willing to take orders from Hoover; and Attorney General Mitchell are booked well in advance. Patrick Jay Hurley, Hoover's very young, very handsome and very energetic Secretary of War, however, is the Beau Brummel of the Cabinet. Hurley studied in Washington, represented the Choctaw Indian Nation in Washington and before he had reached the age of forty-five had made about $15,000,000, chiefly in Washington. Finally, he married tall, blonde and determined Ruth Wilson, daughter of a rear-admiral and from Washington. Hurley, therefore, despite the fact that he entered the Cabinet late, had a running start on the rest of his colleagues, as far as Washington society is concerned. In order to maintain his lead, he took a swank house next to Eugene Meyer's on Crescent Place, and every Wednesday his wife dutifully pours tea for itinerant Oklahomans and any others who may grace her drawing-room. The gathering is dull but politically necessary to Pat's vice-presidential ambitions.

It has been a long time since Oklahoma was honored by having a native son in the Cabinet and the State expects its

Cabinet representative to know his social onions. The neighbors from Tulsa follow every dinner and tea which Ruth and Pat attend and a whole carload of them came up for the first dinner which the Secretary of War gave to the President of the United States. They arrived a day or two earlier in order to rest up before the big event, and although showered with invitations from other less-favored Oklahomans during the two days prior to the party, they declined all of them. If there were any jaded complexions, heavy heads, or dark circles under eyes at the Hurley-Hoover dinner it was an Act of God and no fault of the Oklahoma delegation.

Ruth and Pat Hurley smiled benignly upon their neighbors and did not disclose the fact that when they first came to Washington they had been so in awe of high society that they had rehearsed their entrances and exits, their conversation and their bows, before every big party.

It is not to the Cabinet, however, that the smart hostess of Washington turns for members of officialdom who will give the right touch to her dinner parties. The Senate offers a much wider range, but out of its ninety-six members, only about a dozen are in real demand. They are: Reed of Pennsylvania, Moses of New Hampshire, Tydings of Maryland, Shipstead of Minnesota, Bingham of Connecticut, Johnson of California, Wagner of New York, Capper of Kansas and Bulkley of Ohio.

David Aiken Reed, especially since he built a palace in the neighborhood of Mr. Hoover's S Street home, put murals in his dining room and installed a telephone with a private number, has been in greater social demand than any of his senatorial colleagues.

Reed goes in for society as hard as he goes in for the Senate. He is indefatigable in regard to both. In the winter he dines out, in the spring he spends his Sundays yachting on the Potomac, in the summer he goes to Bar Harbor, and in the fall he shoots ducks. His wife, sweet-tempered and considerate, nurses her senatorial husband like the small boy he sometimes is.

Reed's only social rival is George Moses. Moses lacks the house, the murals and the private telephone, but he has two other assets—his face is not so lugubrious as Reed's nor his conversation so earnest; and, much more important, one can never tell when Moses will be subject to one of his fits of indiscretion and wax vituperative in regard to his chief *bête noir,* Herbert Hoover. Such moments, weeks later, still make a dinner party the talk of the town. Mrs. Moses, silent and self-effacing, wears a look of loyal martyrdom.

Millard Tydings, brilliant bachelor, has been known to offend sedate Georgetown ladies by playing "footie" with them under the table, but among the younger set he remains the Senate's most dined-out member. He also holds the Senate's heart-throb record. He has caused more capital beauties to dream of hooking a senatorial husband than any member of that body in years. One of them even took a trip to Reno with that in mind. Probably the secret of this is the fact that Tydings gives them no encouragement. The thought of him, clad in purple dressing-gown, painting hunting scenes in his attic studio at midnight, is enough to bring out the sacrifice complex in any woman. What could be more useful than to help a lonely Senator mold his great career?

Arthur Capper, sixty-six-year-old widower and millionaire publisher of moral journals, is not only one of the Senate's prime diners-out but probably its chief dancer-out. Debutantes flock around him like lame-ducks around a job. And despite the fact that his fox-trot has a hop in it reminiscent of a gay-nineties two-step, the debs continue to dance with him and to buy new evening slippers.

Robert Johns Bulkley is the Senate's latest contribution to the hostess's insatiable demand for something new in dinner guests. Successful wet senatorial candidate in the dry State of Ohio, he is being touted as Democratic presidential timber, and, as a result, every capital hostess is booking advance space on the Senator's friendship list. As a prosecutor in the capital's latest mystery game—"Murder"—the Senator from Ohio is a washout. The lights are turned out. There is a scream. The lights are turned on again. The prostrate figure of the murdered guest is found lying on the floor and the other guests are lined up for questioning. Then as the *pièce de résistance* of her evening, the hostess brings forth the leading attorney of Ohio and asks him to expose the guilty. He pokes a pudgy finger at each witness and inquires with mild mannered amiability: "Did you commit this crime?"

He has never yet found the criminal.

The House of Representatives, with its four hundred and thirty-five members, proportionately has even less to offer Washington hostesses than the Senate. Topping the list of eligibles are Piatt Andrew and Dick Wigglesworth of Massachusetts, Ruth McCormick of Illinois, Simms of New Mexico, Ruth Bryan Owen of Florida, Dick Aldrich of Rhode Island and Jack Wainwright, Bob Bacon, Ham Fish and Ruth Pratt, all of New York.

Piatt Andrew is the most sought-after member of the House. He is that body's most eligible and elusive bachelor. He has a mansion at Gloucester, Massachusetts, famous for a lounging room reached only by a ladder, which, to insure complete privacy, can be pulled in. His notoriety was increased when Ruth Bryan Owen, just arrived in Washington, was reputed to have thrown roses to him from the gallery of the House. The rumor that there was to be a Republican-Democratic alliance between the Representatives from Massachusetts and Florida has now been shattered.

Mrs. Owen, daughter of William Jennings Bryan, has been played up to Washington hostesses as the Congresswoman with sex appeal. Mrs. Owen is a grandmother. Before reaching the age of discretion, she eloped with a missionary named Leavitt, and later, exquisitely unhappy, was taken by her mother to Egypt where she met and married a British officer, Major Reginald Owen. Her oldest children grew up unaware that they bore the name of Leavitt. Mrs. Owen stays reasonably late at parties, is not a bad dancer and refuted the charge of being the only British subject elected to Congress.

Since her defeat for the United States Senate, the Widow McCormick has consoled herself with introducing a debutante daughter to high society and building a whoopee house in the garden of her Georgetown home, in which she dances with Congressman Simms, another lame-duck. Mrs. McCormick prefers to dine at home rather than at large, and gives intimate dinner parties, to which she invites a mixture of Senators, newspapermen and would-be intellectuals, serving them with tomato-juice cocktails and champagne cider. Chiefly because her late husband, Medill McCormick, was a famous wet, she is the strictest dry in Washington society.

Outside of these cases, the expert hostess finds Capitol Hill a dry and sterile desert. Nor is there more abundant harvest in other official fields. The Army and the Navy move in a social world all their own. Their wealthier members drink mint-juleps on summer evenings at the Chevy Chase Club and the less wealthy do the same thing at the Army, Navy and Marine Corps Country Club. With a few exceptions, their conversation is as inspiring as that of the Army's ex-Chief-of-Staff, General Charles P. Summerall, who, when he sits beside a young and beautiful lady, invariably expounds the glories of a military career.

Among the few exceptions are Admiral William V. Pratt, who is so original in his thinking that he is always about five laps ahead of the State Department and ten ahead of the Navy; General Douglas MacArthur, young, bald, and a great glad-hander, whose promotion to be Chief-of-Staff brought fleeting pangs of pain to the present Mrs. Lionel Atwill (the former Mrs. MacArthur); General Charles Laurie McCawley, charming and diminutive Marine Corps officer; and Colonel Louis McNulty Little, who, with his wife, the former Elsie Cobb Wilson, make one of the most delightful couples in Washington.

With them, although not strictly military, should be included Trubee Davison, and David Sinton Ingalls, Assistant Secretaries of War and the Navy for Aviation. Together with Lou Douglas, lone Congressman from the State of Arizona, they are seen at most of the smart dinner tables and even more frequently in each other's company.

Trubee Davison has started early to do what his late father, partner in the firm of J. P. Morgan, always wanted to do—use his wealth and ability in some public service. As a result, Trubee works at his "little cabinet" job as if it were the most important in the world and the Air Corps is devoted to him. His wife, once Dorothy Peabody, is the daughter of the head of Groton where Trubee went to school, and she has never been able quite to get accustomed to spending money after the manner of those born with silver spoons in their mouths. As a result she requisitions army trucks and soldiers to move her household goods and sends army airplanes from her Long Island home to bring silver she has forgotten to take with her from Washington. She smokes a pipe through preference rather than affectation and is an extremely efficient mother to four small children.

Trubee, sometimes inclined to be as precocious as his six-year-old, has developed the trick of getting himself out of a locked mail-bag, which he will demonstrate when sufficiently urged. Once when his neighbor, Mrs. Maud Torr, had gone off to the movies, leaving her husband, Secretary of the British Embassy, enthralled with the brilliant chit-chat and suppressed desires of Nancy Hoyt, Trubee decided to play the rôle of Protector of the Home. Getting Lou Douglas to drag him, locked inside his mail bag, into the Torr home, Trubee flounced all over the room, upset chairs, knocked down the fire screen trying to extract himself. Finally, red-faced and almost suffocated, Douglas had to extract him. The trick catch on the lock had slipped.

The social sterility of the official field causes the capital's most successful whip-crackers to do a great deal of shopping on the outside. Their constant problem is to find a combination of State Department, diplomatic, congressional, George town and journalistic dinner guests who will put sufficient snap into the evening without precipitating any severe social ructions. Each hostess usually has her own dinner pets, with the result that people find themselves gravitating into groups whose members see increasingly more of one another, and, perhaps as a commentary on their breadth of vision, never seem to be bored.

There are, of course, groups within groups, cliques within cliques, and overlapping of cliques and groups, but probably the three most interesting and well-recognized of these self-gravitating sets are those who until Nick's death played for high stakes under the slap-dash inspiration of Laura Curtis and the Longworths; those who go in for political conversation at the prodding of Mrs. Borden Harriman and Mrs. Frank West; and those who go in for conservative drinking, conservative dancing and conservative love-making when sufficiently chaperoned by the younger Britishers, the Canadians and the H.B.V.'s.

The Curtis-Longworth parties were always wringing wet and usually terminated in poker, although frequently not until Nick had yielded to a demand that he play his violin. Alice and Nick long ago had reached a very amicable understanding that each could go more or less his or her own way, with the result that the two frequently turned up at entirely different parties, or, if they came together, Alice sometimes left long before Nick remembered that somehow or other he had to wield the gavel in the Speaker's chair at twelve o'clock sharp the next morning. This was one of the things that Cissie Patterson upset with her blast against Alice in the Washington *Herald*. Nick used to be a regular visitor at the Patterson du Pont Circle home, but the open attack on his wife was even more than his amiable indifference could tolerate.

Other ladies who move only in the highest circles have equally amicable arrangements worked out with their husbands, provided they still retain such appendages. Among these are Mrs. Truxton Beale, who, although devoted to her aging husband, sometimes leaves him for airplane jaunts over Egypt and the Arabian desert; and Mrs. Tracy Dows, who went off to Europe several years ago a gray-haired, plump, and somewhat sedentary matron, to come back a few months later with golden hair and a vanished waistline. She promptly left her husband in New York, and, except when he comes down for Thanksgiving or Christmas, leads the life of a grass widow, dabbling her fingers into the Washington social stream where it runs hot but not too swift.

Alice Dows and Marie Beale both moved with grace and dignity in the Laura Curtis-Nick Longworth set, and, along with Cornelia Mayo, were sometimes referred to as Nick's girls, although the first two never asked the Speaker's intervention to get them an invitation to a costume ball.

In the same set also move Mr. and Mrs. John Philip Hill, the former being Baltimore's most ardent wet and the man who, by fermenting grape juice in his cellar and daring the prohibition officials to prevent him, won back for the American people their biblical right to make wine out of water.

Not exactly in this group, but not exactly outside it, are two families for whose parties a good many people break their necks to wangle invitations. They are the Henry Leonards, famous for the Butler-Mussolini court martial case, and Mr. and Mrs. Eugene Meyer, the former famous as the only man who never lost his temper with Senator Brookhart.

Eugene Meyer has been a perpetual official-holder ever since the Wilson Administration and he has been an able one. Why he puts up with the senatorial brick-bats that come his way, as a reward for accepting an insignificant salary for doing a $50,000 a year job, is what some of his New York friends cannot understand. The secret is that Meyer has all the money he wants and gets no thrill at all out of making more. His wife, Agnes, goes in for Chinese art, Mayan architecture and dinner-dances, one of which touched off the Gann-Longworth row.

Ellen Warder Leonard, sister of Alice Garrett, American

Ambassadress in Rome, has the most attractive garden in Georgetown, one of the most attractive husbands in Washington, four grandchildren and the patience of Job. Her husband, a one-armed and retired Major in the Marine Corps, can outride, outbluff and outcourt any man between Colorado, where he spends his summers, and Virginia, where he is in constant demand as a horse-show judge. It was Leonard who bluffed Hoover and the State Department out of the Smedley Butler court martial.

A whip-cracker in her own right, Mrs. Edward B. McLean was also once a member of the Poker Players. Now she sits alone at "Friendship," the vast McLean estate on the northwest edge of the city, leads a hermit existence in Florida, or swears out warrants to have her husband prevented from divorcing her in Mexico.

There was a day when two bands imported from New York jazzed alternately at the opposite ends of the McLean ballroom, when several hundred bottles of champagne were opened in an evening and when the most select of social Washington uncertainly danced the New Year into the dawn. There was also a day when Ned McLean dined regularly at the White House, and on such days that he didn't, Warren Gamaliel Harding dined or cocktailed with him at the Little Green House on K Street. There was a day when the Washington *Post* influenced administration policy and brought both Evelyn and Ned power and prestige. Those days are now over. Mrs. McLean still has the Hope diamond but wears it almost never. Ned McLean is rarely seen at the White House and has auctioned off his famous racing stable in Virginia.

The end came with their marital break. Together they were a power in Washington. Diplomats, the State Department, even the White House, feared them. Alone they are nothing —nothing more than divorce and alimony news blurted out on the front page of the McLean newspapers.

\*

LIKE every other social group in the capital, the politico-intellectuals are dominated by widowed ladies bored with New York, San Francisco and Chicago who have settled in Washington to amuse themselves with the profundities of politicians and the jingles of journalists. Probably the most interesting and only semi-serious social group in Washington, it is led by the Widow Harriman, godmother of the Democratic Party, by the Widow West, a newcomer into Democracy who takes it most seriously, and by two such irreconcilable Republicans as the Widows Keep and McCormick.

Daisy Harriman has a disposition so magnanimous that she has seldom been known to say an unkind word about any one except members of the reigning Republican Party. But there are two things Daisy loves almost as much as she does the Democratic Party. These are: to bait Tom Walsh and to give deliciously scrambled dinner parties at which the Republican Administration is dissected piece by piece and pronounced unfit ever again to regain the voters' confidence.

There was a day when Washington expected Daisy Harriman to marry Senator Walsh. There was also a day when Daisy herself thought rather seriously about it. At first it was his mustache which deterred her. It was of the long, weeping-willow variety so fashionable among prospectors who have long been away from both civilization and scissors in the Senator's home state. It used to strain the vegetables from the soup and gather globules of mayonnaise that glistened in the candle-light. Finally Daisy persuaded the Senator to trim it. There is a suspicion among her friends that she achieved this only on the promise that she would marry him and that, after achieving it, she went back on her word.

Walsh was decidedly difficult after this and it took Daisy several years of persuasion to score with him again. Her next goal was his great protruding eyebrows that jutted out from his forehead as sagebrush off a cliff. They gave his eyes a cadaverous effect, and when he hammered on the table and demanded the facts regarding Teapot Dome, it seemed to

Harry F. Sinclair that Walsh was looking at him from a long way off and peering right straight down into his harassed soul.

But Daisy didn't appreciate this, and eventually she took her own scissors and sheared the Senator, as Samson was shorn of yore.

Walsh is milder and fairly manageable now. Occasionally, when Daisy has over-exploited him for the benefit of her dinner guests, he sulks a little and boycotts her parties. But for the most part, he performs grimly and dutifully and loves it. A strange couple, they have all the affection for each other that a purely platonic friendship can have without the chafing of married life.

Gravitating in the same politico-intellectual orbit is Birne West, wealthy California widow, beautiful, witty, greedily on the lookout for unexploited dinner guests, a specialist at mixing soup and Senators, always able to get the maximum kick out of her own jokes; Mrs. Frederick (Florence) Keep, gentle, considerate, gracious, with one of the few well-stocked cellars in Washington, and a sister, Miss Mabel Boardman, whom the Prince of Wales once mistook for his royal mother; Adolph and Mary Miller, the former solemn and always ready to expound on the Federal Reserve Board on which he sits; a scattering of newspapermen—the Oulahans, the Hards and the Ned Lowrys plus the Edward Burlings, whose log cabin up the Potomac is the rendezvous every Sunday for most of the above.

Most of them will not admit they are intellectuals. They affect a sense of humor about life, but if they ever got frank with themselves they would confess to a considerable amount of intellectual egocentricism. And, as a matter of fact, they come closest to being the only intellectuals able to exist in the rarefied atmosphere of social Washington.

*

Social life among the younger set is never static in the capital. It ebbs and flows. Debutantes bud, blossom, marry

and move away, to come back years later when they are
divorced, to settle down and eventually take over the place of
some exalted society whip-cracker who has retired from the
ring. In the same way, the fledglings of the State Department's white-spat corps are ordered to Callao, Singapore and
Cape Town, to come back years later as always available last-
minute dinner guests for distracted hostesses. In general, however, it is safe to assume that the perennial Leander Goodhart
McCormick and his charming wife Janet will always be on
hand, and that the really select members of the younger crowd
will be dominated by the attachés of the British Embassy, the
Canadian Legation and the H.B.V.'s, which used to be considered very shocking and very secret initials, but which now
are blurted out across any dinner table as the "High Bosomed
Virgins."

# CHAPTER TWO

## STARCHED FUTILITY

*FROM* the point of view of the Diplomatic Corps, Washington is the most unique capital in the world.

It is, for instance, the only capital where the Minister of Guatemala is more important to a foreign office than the Ambassador of Spain.

It is, for instance, the only capital where the Minister of Nicaragua is more important to a foreign office than the envoys from Finland, Latvia, Esthonia, Lithuania and Denmark, all put together.

It is for instance, the only capital where the Minister of Panama may sit absolutely quiet in Washington and receive a telegram from his Supreme Court asking him to assume the Presidency of his country.

The secret of this, of course, is the United States' Economic Empire to the south. The total number of American dollars invested in the banana and coffee plantations of infinitesimal Guatemala just about equal those invested in the mines and street railways of much vaster and more populated Spain. And, in addition, Guatemala is much nearer the Panama Canal. Spain may suffer a revolution and it will not even occur to the State Department to send cruisers and marines. But if revolution breaks out in Guatemala, not only does the State Department immediately suffer a gunboat complex, but it also notifies the revolutionary leader that he cannot become President.

There are five other Central American countries, plus three in the Caribbean, plus twelve on the South American continent and Mexico, whose envoys get flowers, fruit and polite messages every time their President has a birthday, they leave on a vacation, or their wives give birth to twins.

All this, of course, is a mere matter of business routine. After the State Department closes its doors at four-thirty, its socially minded young men, with the exception of Francis White, who cannot help himself, are to be found, not in the homes of Latin-American envoys, whom they fête by day, but cocktailing and dining among those diplomats who seldom have to concern themselves with affairs of state but are skilled in saying the right word at the right time.

Washington's Diplomatic Corps, therefore, might be divided into two parts:

Those who dine out and those who dine at home.

Or to paraphrase, the Corps might be divided into those who dine out and those who work.

This, however, would not be strictly accurate. There would have to be noted such distinguished exceptions as:

> The British Ambassador, Sir Ronald Lindsay, who is invited out both because he is charming and because he represents His Majesty's far-flung Empire, and yet, despite all that, manages, in a dull, British sort of way, to turn out a reasonable amount of work.
>
> The Cuban Ambassador, Orestes Ferrara, who is invited out because of his wit rather than the importance of his country, but who none the less works early in the morning and late into the night.
>
> The Bolivian Minister, Diez de Medina, whom scarcely any one invites out, and who, having no work to do, manages to get involved in all kinds of remarkable and compromising situations.

For purposes of strict accuracy, therefore, it is necessary to divide the Diplomatic Corps into four groups, which, except when they attend the Secretary of State's breakfast on New Year's Day or the Diplomatic Reception at the White House, have about as much in common as Dolly Gann and Alice Longworth. They are:

The Smart Set, which includes the important European envoys who have to be invited out, regardless of their wealth or their wives, plus a lot of lesser lights who are asked out in order to counterbalance the deadheads and give a little leavening to the party.

The Latin Americans, whose leading Ambassadors rate just as high officially but not socially as the Big Five of Europe.

The Asiatics, who keep very much to themselves.

The Balkan, Near East and the Border States, beneath whose appearance of boredom run some of the most bizarre lives in Washington.

*

UNTIL the British Empire becomes infinitely more down-at-the-heel than it now is, its Ambassador, no matter whether he be prosaic or platitudinous, always will be the most dominant figure in the Diplomatic Corps. So to-day, the British Empire, still being one with which the United States has been able to achieve only paper naval parity, Sir Ronald Lindsay, outranks, in power and prestige, every other Ambassador in Washington. He achieves this despite the fact that Ambassador Tellez of Mexico, Dean of the Corps, is a much abler man; despite the fact that Sir Ronald is very new and a little green; despite the fact that he is deaf; and despite the fact that his wife, because of her illness, has an unhappy way of stepping on people's pet theories. The answer is that the British Empire is simply too powerful to take a back seat.

Sir Ronald would be a distinguished and dominant diplomat whatever country he represented. Somewhat less charming but far more canny than his predecessor, Sir Esme Howard, Lindsay would be the last one in the world to answer a letter written by a Virginia dry promising to import no more liquor for the British Embassy—a promise, which, although sincerely given by poor old Sir Esme, never got him any credit even from the drys, due to the fact that his irate undersecretaries let slip the fact that his cellar was stocked with much more than he could ever drink up before his retirement.

Nor would Sir Ronald Lindsay ever make the mistake of leaving Washington for the North Shore, as did Sir Esme in 1927, just on the eve of a naval conference which, due partially to his absence, was to make Anglo-American history by marring Anglo-American friendship. Lindsay has made only one break so far and that was a very minor and rather amusing one which occurred when he met Drew Pearson, of the Baltimore *Sun,* in the halls of the State Department, and, thinking he was an assistant of Secretary Stimson's, told him about the very confidential steps Great Britain and the United States were taking to bring France and Italy into the London Naval Conference. Pearson never published the news until some days later, when he received permission from both Ambassador Lindsay and the State Department, but for the moment, Sir Ronald was as embarrassed as a third secretary who has spilled ice cream down the neck of his Ambassadress.

Lindsay is a Scotsman whose six feet eight inches, in Highland kilts and bare knees, make a rare figure of a man. Washington has never seen him thus garbed, but it would like to. He has a great drooping mustache of the Senator Walsh type before Daisy Harriman induced him to trim it, and his deafness makes him incline his massive shoulders slightly nearer the earth in order to catch the words of those who would talk with him from below.

Lady Lindsay is a nervous and irritable lady who spent one of the hottest summers Washington has ever known moving furniture to the new British Embassy on Massachusetts Avenue and telling curious people who insisted on getting early glimpses of the establishment to "please do not track up the rugs" or "please don't move those chairs," with the result that by midsummer she had to be taken to Long Island in an ambulance.

The British Embassy, until a Socialist Government came into power, used to be the social arbiter of Washington, and a bid to dine there was more coveted by some than an invitation to the White House. Those days are now about as antiquated as the White House cocktail parties of the Harding administration, due not only to the advent of the Labor Party but also to the departure of Sir Adrian Bailey and Henry Hopkinson, who, having no great talents in any other direction, concentrated upon dinners and debutantes. The British Embassy for the most part is now a cold and silent tomb perched upon the hill, to be lighted up only for such formal and stodgy occasions as diplomacy requires.

The other leaders of the Smart Set within the Diplomatic Corps include von Prittwitz of Germany, de Martino of Italy, Claudel of France, and, until the hurried exit of Alfonso, Padilla of Spain. Next to Claudel, the most celebrated of these is the small and wiry little personage who bears the name Nobile Giacomo de Martino, Ambassador of the Royal Italian Government.

The type of celebrity Martino has achieved is vastly different from Claudel's. It verges on notoriety. He won it, first, through the Fascist League of North America and its persecution of Italians in the United States; second, through Major General Smedley D. Butler, U.S.M.C.

Like many men of small stature, Martino makes up for his height by his pugnacious persistence. Long before General Butler put him on the map with the general public, Martino had come to have the same relation to State Department officials as a mosquito to a malarial patient.

He called at the Department on every possible occasion and pretext. If he could find no pretext, he called to chat about the weather. It is no exaggeration to say that he called and still calls more frequently than all the other members of the Diplomatic Corps put together. He subscribes to a most comprehensive clipping service and whenever he finds that an editor, even in Sioux City or Okmulgee, is maligning his

Fascist chief, Martino trots down to the State Department to complain. The fact that the State Department's reply is always the same—"The United States has no censorship as you do in Italy"—does not deter Martino a bit. He always comes back for more.

The State Department, therefore, did not show one glimmer of surprise when Martino turned up one morning with a clipping from the Philadelphia *Record* reporting that the most distinguished officer in the Marine Corps had branded the Dictator of Italy as a hit-and-run driver. The *Record* happens to have the smallest circulation of any Philadelphia newspaper. If Martino had not brought the clipping down to the State Department, probably no more than a mere handful of people would have noticed Butler's accusation. After he called, several million became firmly convinced that Mussolini did run over a child and did exclaim: "What is one life in the affairs of a State?"

But for Martino that clipping was a great opportunity. At last he had the State Department where he wanted it. No longer could Bill Castle turn him off with the reminder that there was no censorship in the United States. This was a commissioned officer in the service of the United States who had spoken. It was not only a great opportunity, but it was heaven-sent. The Fascist Consul in New York had been dimming Martino's luster. He had been getting credit in Rome for being the real Ambassador to the United States. Martino needed some such incident as this, and, sparing no cable costs, he promptly wired his Fascist Chief all the details.

No one, therefore, was more pleased with himself than the persistent little Ambassador when he came to the State Department to receive Secretary Stimson's note of "deep regret." He fell all over himself in his haste to get to the cable office and put the results of his victory on the wires to Rome.

His smug self-satisfaction lasted but two days. The court martial ordered by the Navy Department proved a boomerang. It hit back at Mussolini with a thousand times the force of the original Butler speech. It stripped away all of the kudos Martino had stored up for himself in Rome. It made people believe that Mussolini really was the bad man General Butler said he was.

Given facts like these, Martino did what he has always done. He called at the State Department. He expressed the view that as far as Italy was concerned the incident was not only "closed but forgotten." A court martial, he said, would be highly embarrassing. Mr. Stimson did the rest. Ambassador Martino achieved at least one victory. The court martial was dropped.

\*

BETWEEN Friedrich W. von Prittwitz und Gaffron, Ambassador of Germany, and the amiable Otto Kiep, his Counselor, there was a rivalry that they scarcely took the trouble to conceal.

The Ambassador, sometimes called "von Nittwitz" by his less appreciative admirers, was awarded the Washington post in return for the many hours and days spent bowing low over the hand of Frau Stresemann. Frau Stresemann's husband, however, has now passed on to a place where he can no longer be Foreign Minister of Germany, and Von Prittwitz must stand on his own two feet.

Amiable Otto Kiep knew this probably as well as any one —perhaps better than Von Prittwitz. And, therefore, Otto, despite a wife who has been known to take him off a ballroom floor for cheek-dancing with a beautiful matron, continued to be amiable and to throw dinners famous for their roast goose, red cabbage, and Rhine wine.

And when the Ambassador went away on vacation—which he did regularly and at some length, Amiable Otto was in his element. He raked up armfuls of distinguished German visitors to present at the White House. He sent lengthy cables to the Foreign Office, reporting in detail what President Hoover told each visitor. And he sent even lengthier cables reporting what the American people, the American press, the American State Department and the American Diplomatic Corps were thinking and saying about Germany in general, and about Amiable Otto Kiep in particular. The Embassy's cable bills increased about threefold when Kiep took charge; but why should he worry when each cable was a step toward his greatest ambition—the under-Secretaryship of the Foreign Office.

Or so he thought.

His father-in-law was one of Prussia's prosperous barons of big business. His brother had designed the German grey-hounds, Bremen and Europa. He himself had been offered a $60,000 job with a German-American business house. Nothing, apparently, could block the onward march of his ambition.

But something did. Either Von Prittwitz was more powerful than any one dreamed, or else Kiep's cable bills were higher than the Foreign Office could stomach. At any rate, he was demoted to be Consul General in New York, where he pretends to be highly pleased with an East Side pent house, submits reports which have to be approved by his arch-enemy, the Ambassador, and takes frequent and wistful trips to see his old friends in Washington.

The Ambassador is young and looks younger than he is. He has a young and attractive wife, and they have a young daughter. They make an attractive-appearing couple and if they were not so shy they would not be unattractive to talk to. As a glad-hander, the Ambassador is a washout. This is a calamity, because his predecessor, the late Von Maltzan, was an adept at this art, and his rival, Amiable Otto, has torn several pages out of Maltzan's book. Probably the unhappiest moments Von Prittwitz ever spent in Washington were when he attempted to glad-hand newspapermen at a beer *abend* and had to submit to the embrace and heavy-laden breathing of the most bibulous star in Hearst's diadem, while he expounded on the good-fellowship of the German people, despite their alleged atrocities in Belgium.

Whether he is responsible for it or not, Von Prittwitz heads the most efficient Embassy in Washington. No article unfavorable to Germany is written without the Embassy spotting it and approaching the author, if he is approachable, with a dinner or luncheon invitation. Rudolf Leitner, an Austrian, is unquestionably the brains of the Embassy, being ably supported by Emil Baer and Johann Lohmann. The staff is one of the hardest working and least social in the capital.

Probably the opposite is true of the Spanish Embassy, which, as before noted, is about as important to the State Department as the Guatemalan Legation, but which maintains eight full-fledged secretaries and attachés, as against Guatemala's two. The answer is that Spanish prestige requires an Embassy and, therefore, also, the military attachés, naval attachés and all the social personnel and paraphernalia that go with it.

Despite all its trappings, the Spanish Embassy is pleasantly and naturally social, and probably will continue to be just as much so under a republic as under a monarchy. Ambassador Padilla had little to do except look over his Madrid cable every morning, twirl his black mustache and announce excitedly: "Spain is quiet." Once in a long while he went down to the State Department to denounce the Treasury Department's restrictions against Spanish cork or to complain bitterly to Bill Castle that Spain should have been a charter member of the Kellogg-Briand Outlawry of War Society. Two or three times each winter he sallied forth to the Metropolis for an opening of the New York opera.

His one really great accomplishment was in forcing the State Department, after one hundred and ten years of obstinacy, to promise damages for Andrew Jackson's raid into West Florida in 1814, when Florida was then sovereign Spanish territory.

But on such rare occasions as Senor Don Alejandro was thus occupied, the social life of the Embassy ran smoothly and charmingly under the guidance of his son and two daughters, of whom Rosa, the eldest, was one of the most attractive girls in Washington. They gave dull and formal dinner parties in

the winter and made up for it in the summer by doing the
devil's dip at Glen Echo or staging midnight parties around
the fountain that cools the Embassy patio. After all—Spanish
temperament is very warm—and it has been a long time since
the war of 1898.

\*

THERE are numerous diplomats who wedge their way into the
Smart Set, not through the weight and prestige of the governments they serve but through: one, the power of their
money: two, the charm of their personalities: or three, the at-
traction of their reputations. Representative of these three
categories in their respective order are Count Szechenyi of
Hungary, Michael MacWhite of the Irish Free State, and
Davila of Rumania.

Laszlo Szechenyi, Scots-Hungarian, with more of the Mag-
yar in him than the Scot, counts diplomatically only because he married Gladys Vanderbilt and her accompanying
millions. Heavy jowled, always with a black patch over one
eye, Szechenyi is the most sinister-looking figure in the Diplomatic Corps, but one who, when sufficiently imbued with
the spirit of the evening, has been known to doff his tail coat,
drape a rug around his portly hips and imitate a bonny Scot
clad in native tartan dancing the Highland Fling.

Szechenyi is the leader of a little group of diplomats, who,
headed by the Red-baiting Bill Castle, have taken a solemn
vow to wage unceasing international guerilla warfare against
radicals. Szechenyi it was who prompted the State Department to bar for so many years the harmless Count Karolyi
who later won the pity of lecture-loving old ladies when
Secretary Stimson finally admitted him to the United States.
And Szechenyi it was again who, when fourteen Jewish working girls came over from Baltimore to parade in front of
his legation, jumped into his high-powered roadster and dis-
appeared down Sixteenth Street.

Michael MacWhite has no mission in the United States

other than to exercise his personality, and this he does to the credit and glory of the Irish Free State. MacWhite is one of those engaging individuals with the usual Irish smile and a frankness that is rare even in an Irishman. When, as a member of the British Empire Delegation, he represented the Irish Free State at the Geneva Naval Conference in 1927, he remarked to an American journalist:

"This is the only time the British and you Yankees have sat down at a conference table side by side and the Yanks haven't been licked. I hope ye keep it up."

As a representative of the Irish Free State at the League of Nations for many years, MacWhite always refused to use English. Whenever he addressed the League Assembly, as he frequently did, he used French, because, as he explained it, "I can't speak my own language, and I'll be damned if I'll speak English."

Such a man performs exactly the duties the Free State Government and Irish-American Societies want an Irish Minister to perform, and as a result he is constantly on tour.

Charles A. Davila is socially there. As to how he got there, there are various stories. Some attribute his arrival to the contrast of his brown shoulders with his snow white bathing suit as he lounges in the sand at Bailey's Beach. Some say it is the same charm which won for him a betrothal with Belle Baruch, daughter of Bernard Baruch, or again the charm which beguiled the New York chorus lady who later cost him such embarrassing litigation.

At any rate, there can be no question that Davila has a fascinating reputation and that this reputation wins for him a place, albeit not the most sought-after place, but, nevertheless, a very refulgent place in Washington's diplomatic and social life.

Davila happened to come to Washington because as a member of a Rumanian financial mission in Paris, he wooed and won—temporarily, at least—Miss Belle Baruch, whose father was one of the monied mainstays of the Wilson Administration. Miss Baruch was not satisfied with the prospect of marrying a mere financial attaché. She was interested in bigger game, and, so the story goes, promised to wed the young Rumanian if he bagged a major diplomatic post. Davila promptly telegraphed Bucharest, reporting that he was engaged to the daughter of the influential Mr. Baruch and suggested that in view of the American prestige, which would undoubtedly accrue through this alliance, the legation in Washington should be his. Either the telegram was garbled or else the Foreign Office did not know its United States Senate, for Bucharest decided that any one who married the daughter of the chairman of the Senate Foreign Relations Committee certainly should be sent to Washington. Later, Cretziano, who objected to being ousted from his comfortable post by such a youngster, had the pleasure of writing to the Foreign Office somewhat as follows:

"I beg to inform you that Senator Borah, Chairman of the Foreign Relations Committee, has no children. It seems incredible, therefore, that the newly appointed Minister is to be married to his daughter."

In the end, Miss Baruch let Davila down. The marriage has never come off. There have been constant rumors of an announcement, but so far the rumors have borne no crop and Washington is beginning to wonder just what happened. The most likely explanation is that Miss Baruch became peeved over the triangular story of Davila, the chorus girl and the ring.

It happened this way: Davila suggested to a lady with a willing disposition that she go out and buy herself a trinket —a ring, perhaps—anything reasonable. The lady went out, but on the way consulted a male friend who was experienced in these matters, and received the suggestion that she borrow from him a ring belonging to another woman to whom he had advanced $500. The lady with the willing disposition was then to collect from Davila to the tune of $1,000 and bring the ring back. All went well except for one hitch. The lady with the willing disposition did not bring the ring back at all. She kept it. Shortly thereafter, its original owner went to the male friend who was experienced in these matters, placed $500 in his hands and demanded her bauble.

The whole thing came to light when the latter lady became overly insistent and sued Davila, as the original giver, for the return of her property.

The incident vexed only one person more than it did Miss Baruch. He was Carlos Davila, Ambassador of Chile, whose photograph appeared in the newspapers instead of that of Davila, the Rumanian.

\*

THE line of demarcation between the Smart Set which dines out and the Latin Americans who work at home is not a straight one. It wavers in the cases of Ambassador Tellez of Mexico, Davila of Chile, Ferrara of Cuba and Amoral of Brazil. The first three are men of exceptional ability, considerable charm, and represent countries whose good will is supremely important to the Latin-American policy of the United States. Ambassador Gurgel do Amoral differed from them only in that his duties never sat very heavily upon his shoulders. He would rather feed his cats than read dispatches from Rio. In fact, he would almost rather feed his cats than make love, which any one who knows Amoral's past may consider an extreme statement.

The Ambassador is a colorful, soulful figure who moved with starched precision across Washington's official stage. He is charmingly, even naïvely, of the *vieille noblesse*. He bows exquisitely from the waist. His pet abominations are motorcycles and flies. In these, his maturer years, his chief love is cats.

Amoral's affection for cats began as a small child. His father preferred dogs. His mother favored cats. Gurgel, torn between two desires, finally decided that cats needed protection from their enemies. His mother's pet cat, Nyssah, was torn to death by two dogs when she lost her balance and fell from the wall of the Amoral home in Rio. Another pet, Bilontra, was instantly killed by a Great Dane. Saddened by their fate, young Amoral determined to be the champion and protector of all persecuted pussies in the future. He has kept his word. In Hyde Park, London, two of the Ambassador's cats rest under marble slabs. In Berlin a granite shaft adorned with a medallion in bronze commemorates a cat named Menina. When, in reward for Amoral's too great loyalty to the late Government of Brazil, the revolutionists demoted him to Tokyo, Flit, his pet pussy, went with him.

Only two rules govern Amoral's feline existence: no cat shall eat mice, and no cat has more than one life.

*

DURING that hectic period prior to 1923, when Charles Evans Hughes and Charles Beecher Warren were trying to jockey Mexico out of the victories won by her revolution in return for American recognition, there sat in the Mexican Embassy in Washington a black-haired, black-eyed youngster named Manuel C. Tellez, who, as far as Mexico was concerned, ran this end of the show.

Finally, after Hughes backed down, and—without a settlement of the petroleum or agrarian controversy—recognized Mexico, this youngster was selected to stay on in the Embassy at Washington as Ambassador. That selection nearly provoked a social revolution in Mexico City. The Washington post was looked upon as a prize political plum. A dozen or more politicians, some of them powerful, were clamoring for it as just reward for their aid to Plutarco Calles and the Revolution. But Calles wanted a man who knew how to handle the State Department and, despite the youth of the nominee, despite the clamor in Mexico City, Calles stuck to his original decision.

Two years passed—two years of bitter controversy. The irate and irascible Frank B. Kellogg had written note after note —all private—to his Ambassador in Mexico City, James R. Sheffield. They were filled with invective. Sheffield answered back in kind. Suddenly the notes fell into the hands of the Mexican Government. Tellez brought them down to the State Department and politely handed them back to Mr. Kellogg. The latter raged. His face was crimson. He claimed the notes were forgeries. Tellez knew they were not. Privately, Kellogg suspected Tellez of stealing them. He ordered every scrap of waste paper burned before it left the State Department. He ordered an investigation of his clerks, his diplomatic couriers, his translators. Tellez was one of the most suspected men in Washington. Members of the State Department scarcely would speak to him. Kellogg handed him a note, announcing that Mexico was on trial before the world. But he stayed on.

To-day, Ambassador Tellez—Dean of the Diplomatic Corps —still a young man—stands at the head of the line when the diplomats greet the President on New Year's morning. He is the first to enter the dining-room at almost every official dinner. He outranks the Senate, the Cabinet, the Secretary of State, and the Speaker of the House of Representatives.

All of which may be mere mush to some people, but to the State Department it means that the youngster who has won every diplomatic joust with the Colossus of the North is still guarding the Rio Grande.

*

ARGENTINA, most powerful nation of Latin America, ought to have in Washington an Ambassador of the Tellez type. It has not. Manuel Malbran is weak, flabby and full of vague ideas about powerful protests he expects some day to make to the State Department about the tariff on meat, wheat and flaxseed, but never effectually does. He is a career diplomat of the Latin-American type, which means an AA rating for phlegmatic inertia. Career diplomats of any nationality are bad enough, but the Latin-American variety mixes all the laziness of the professional dilettante with none of the social charm of his European colleague.

Malbran is now on his second tour of duty in Washington. The first tour ended in a way that few people know about and Malbran hates to recall. His pay was cut off by President Irigoyen; no diplomatic dispatches were routed to him by the Argentine Foreign Office; and he was left high and dry in Washington, not knowing whether he was Ambassador or totem pole.

An Ambassador does not object, usually, to being transferred, and sometimes, provided he can rise up in his wrath and get a lot of publicity for himself by a war of words with his home government, he does not even object to resigning. But to be totally ignored, to have the State Department take pity on your ignorance by sending you copies of the correspondence received direct from Buenos Aires, to have all your colleagues smile knowingly behind your back—that is the worst fate that can ever befall a diplomat. And that was the fate that befell Malbran. Loyal career man that he is, however, he has now swallowed his pride and is back in Washington working once more for the glory of his country and $25,000 a year.

Among the other Latin-American diplomats the most outstanding are the suave and urbane Don Manuel de Freyre y Santander, Ambassador of Peru, who needs only a monocle to make him the most complete Englishman in the United States, and who, although very new to Washington, is rapidly becoming one of the social satellites of the Corps; the ashen-faced Diez de Medina, of Bolivia, described by one of his colleagues as having the rank of Minister, the brains of a third secretary and the habits of a military attaché; and the tall and gawky Juan B. Sacasa, Minister of Nicaragua.

Sacasa had one of the greatest triumphs of his life when

he walked into the White House to present his credentials as Minister to the United States. Three years before that triumphal entry, Sacasa, then Vice President of Nicaragua, had cooled his heels in the ante-room and corridors of the State Department for months trying to persuade its officials that he, rather than Chamorro, the revolutionist, should be recognized as President of Nicaragua. He failed to get anything more than sympathy, and returned to Nicaragua. En route he stopped in Mexico and, having become friendly in Washington with Ambassador Tellez, he got from President Calles more concrete encouragement—arms and ammunition. The rest of the story was blazoned black and bold in the headlines of the newspapers of that day—how Frank B. Kellogg sent fifteen warships and five thousand marines to quell Sacasa's forces, and how Henry L. Stimson finally went as peacemaker, pledging supervision of the election by which Sacasa's Liberals won a sweeping electoral victory, Jose Moncada becoming President, and Sacasa, Minister to Washington.

The Latin-American members of the Diplomatic Corps for the most part are able men and work hard. They have to. Next to the President and one or two Cabinet officers, they hold the most important post in their government. They represent their nation of one or two or perhaps ten million people at the capital of the mightiest nation in the world, a nation which controls most of the world's gold, a nation whose tariff may overnight ruin their export trade, a nation whose State Department may cause revolution by the mere refusal of a loan, a nation which has proclaimed a Monroe Doctrine by which it sets itself up as the protector of all the Western Hemisphere, a nation which, in short, holds all but the three largest governments of Latin America literally in the palm of its hand.

No wonder then that Washington's Latin-American Diplomatic Corps works hard. No wonder, also, that when they seek recreation they herd together, rarely mingling with their European colleagues or the State Department's social satellites. A powerful enemy develops the herd instinct.

*

FROM a social, political and economic point of view, most of the diplomats representing the Asiatic, Balkan, and so-called Border States might just as well pack their rugs in moth balls, discharge their cooks, and cut down their national budgets by the cost of one Washington Legation per year. Except for the telephone girls in the Hotel Mayflower, almost nobody in the United States, not even the State Department, knows that there is an Albanian Minister in Washington. The same is true of the Latvian, the Lithuanian and the Finn, except that they lack even a following of telephone girls, unless they have been more subversive about it than most people guess. The same would also be true of the Siamese, were it not for the fact that a maladroit policeman seized a truckload of Siamese liquor about two years ago and kept the poor little Minister, Major General Prince Amoradat Kridakara, on the front pages so long that he scarcely had time to recover before the arrival of his King for eye treatment subjected him to a fresh deluge of publicity.

Not even the Japanese Ambassador is seen very much in Washington, despite the fact that he is a most charming individual. As far as prestige goes, Katsuji Debuchi is a big shot. He is invited to all the dinners that he should be invited to, but to few of such *intime* affairs as those at which the Widow McCormick or Daisy Harriman drag in the men who are really doing things and discuss the latest skulduggery of the capital.

The staff of the Japanese Embassy is the biggest in Washington. This is because the intricacies of the Japanese language make typewriting impossible and it is necessary for an immense retinue of secretaries to spend hours each day painting English into Japanese. As a result, the staff is so big that it could spend the entire winter more or less dining among its own members and not be fed up with quite all of them. Whether Ambassador Debuchi spends his time that way nobody knows. But unless naval negotiations or a Russo-Chinese row in Manchuria bring him out into the open he makes himself as scarce as the ground-hog in February.

Dr. C. C. Wu,* Debuchi's colleague from the Asiatic mainland, is much more in the limelight. This is both because the limelight brightens his soul as sunlight builds bonny babies and because he is more at home in Washington than in Shanghai, Peking or Canton.

Old Wu-ting-fang, the first Minister China sent to Washington and who delighted its inhabitants by regularly parading a long blue mandarin coat and a pig-tail down Connecticut Avenue, brought with him his son, C. C. Wu, then a mischievous Chinese youngster of eight. Young Wu attended Western High School, threw snowballs at its windows, and came to be as much of a rough-and-tumble American as any one in his class. Now that he has come back to Washington, he tells gullible women's clubs about China's modern progress in a slow American drawl, makes perennial trips to persuade Secretary Stimson to abolish extra-territoriality and is one of the few diplomats in the capital who is a fair match for the newspapermen who beleaguer him at the entrance of the State Department.

Ahmet Muhtar, Ambassador of Turkey, has been a great disappointment to the pious wives of all Congressmen who wanted to meet a man with a harem. Not only does he lack the four wives prescribed by Mohammed for all good Moslems, but he has no wife at all. Furthermore, he is a washout as a table companion as far as most congressional wives are concerned, for he talks about as much English as they do French.

* Dr. Wu has now resigned in protest against American shipments of munitions to the Chinese Government to be used against his fellow citizens in Canton.

Just across the street from the Turkish Embassy, however, is one of the most interesting foreign establishments in the capital. It gives no official receptions; it sends no envoys to the State Department. Its occupants are not registered in the Diplomatic List. But occasionally they do throw a dinner, with much caviar and vodka to a guest list which is the most carefully selected in town. And its Ambassador, unofficial though he may be, is unquestionably one of the ablest in or out of the Diplomatic Corps.

The Information Bureau of the Soviet Union has no diplomatic rating, but it is called, by those who know anything about it, the Soviet Embassy. Boris E. Skvirsky, its chief, is an employee of the Soviet Foreign Office and draws his salary from it just as does any Soviet Ambassador to any other part of the world. He came to Washington ten years ago as the representative of the Far Eastern Republic of Siberia, in an effort to put Soviet Siberia's claims before the Washington Conference. Although he failed in that, he has been here ever since, and this fact alone, taking into consideration the Red Menace investigation of Ham Fish and the anti-Russian complex of the State Department, is sufficient indication of his success.

Probably because they have nothing else to do, the envoys of the Balkan and Border States—those who are neither in nor out of high society—lead the most bizarre lives in Washington. The Persian and the Albanian, although ostensibly with little in common except Charley Hart who has been American Minister to both countries, have the reputation of staging parties equalled only along Broadway or the Bosporus. Bey, the old Egyptian Minister, is still being mourned by the capital's greatest guzzlers. Charalambos Simopoules, the Greek, and his wife, play for the highest stakes in town and are fully able, if they wish—and some of their friends ruefully contend that they do wish—to make enough each week to pay the upkeep of their legation.

Faik Konitza, the Albanian, and Mirza Davoud Khan

Meftah, the Persian, used to begin their parties very quietly, sometimes with an afternoon picnic in Rock Creek Park, featured by large onion sandwiches and little Persian pickled onions. Perhaps it was the mixture of onions and champagne or the unusual union of Albania and Persia, but as the afternoon and evening wore on, the parties gathered momentum and buoyancy.

Konitza now is a lonely man. His companion-in-relieving-the-monotony-of-the-Washington-vacuum has gone back to Persia. The why and wherefore of his going was sad and shrouded in mystery. Mirza Davoud Khan Meftah had an enemy—a young Persian of royal blood who was attached to his own staff. The attachment was purely nominal, for Mozaffar Mirza Firouz never did any work and it was over this that the two fell out. The stories of what subsequently happened differ, but this—for what it is worth—is the Minister's version of it.

Young Firouz wrote to the United States Customs officials stating that the Minister was taking advantage of his diplomatic immunity to smuggle opium into the United States. He even informed the customs authorities that a consignment of the drug was arriving at such and such a date. Then, according to Mirza, young Firouz had his friends in Persia send a package of opium to the Minister. The package arrived, was seized by the customs, and Mirza was confronted with the evidence. He pleaded a frame up and was recalled, together with Firouz. And so passed from the diplomatic stage one of those benign and soulful figures which Washington always associated with pickled onions and rouge inscriptions on the starched bosoms of sleeping plenipotentiaries.

## CHAPTER THREE

## THE PRESIDENT

No man ever came to the Presidency with a greater opportunity for constructive and courageous administration than Herbert Hoover.

The national temper, the economic and political situation were over-ripe for a vigorous and positive leadership. The country was ready, as it had rarely been, for a man of principle, purpose, and will.

Eight years of the criminalities, puerile mediocrity, and reactionary do-nothingness of the Harding and Coolidge régimes had crystallized a deep urge in the national consciousness for a man of really first class caliber. The country was sated with the pettiness, the tragic weaknesses, and the asinine posturing of its leaders. It wanted some one it could be honestly proud of.

There were many reasons for it to believe that Herbert Hoover was that man.

Liberal leaders had acclaimed him. Far and wide he was hailed as an executive and a doer. He was not a professional politician. He did not come from a class that produced politicians. He was an engineer who apparently had done well at his work.

His public service was heroic. The whole world had applauded his great humanitarian exploits. He had fed starving millions, succored whole nations. He had taken a small, little-known department, and made it the most potent and widely advertised agency of the government.

True, little of the man himself was known. Long periods of his life were utterly blank, except for studiously vague explanations. His business career and operations were carefully guarded and elaborately obscured.

About his various food administrations there was also much that was highly debatable. Farmers accused him of having deliberately favored grain operators as against their interests. Even Old Guard Republican leaders, such as Representative William R. Wood, of Indiana, Chairman of the Republican Congressional Campaign Committee, had risen on the floors of Congress and bitterly assailed his management.

In Europe it was related of his food administration that he and his subordinates had used vital food resources, given by a generous people to feed starving women and children, as a weapon to crush the uprisings of oppressed masses throwing off the yokes of the masters who had precipitated the catastrophic World War.

There was the fact also that while making the Department of Commerce a mighty instrument of trade and business he had sat silent and unperturbed among Cabinet colleagues whose gross crimes and corruptions are unparalleled in the history of the country.

But all this was brushed aside in the trusting belief that he was a man of action, of broad vision, of force of character and mind. Not even a Presidential campaign, significant only in its grim evasion and covert bigotry, could dissipate the profound confidence in his inherent integrity and ability.

The American people believed in Herbert Hoover, the hero. They believed in him as the Great Engineer, the Great Administrator, the Great Humanitarian, the Great Idealist. They believed in him so earnestly that he was able to do the impossible in Presidential history: come back after having been discarded by the politicians.

The people elected him President by the greatest majority in a national election. They installed him in the White House, cast in a lofty rôle. They were ready to follow him in a courageous, independent, enlightened administration. He had but to lead the way.

The scene, the rôle, the play, even the audience was his own making. All that was needed was the courage and intellectual integrity to live up to the personality he had the genius to imprint on the public mind. Nothing could have stopped him.

In less than two years after he had taken office he had fully revealed the true quality of his character. He wrote the record fast and for all time. It is to be found in every phase of his administration.

He began his term with a Congress overwhelmingly Republican in both branches. Twenty months later a disillusioned and bitter electorate swept these majorities away and placed the control of the national legislature in the hands of his opponents.

He took over the reins of a party flushed with victory and high in morale. To-day, it is furtive, besmirched, and disorganized, filling the Nation with the stench of its Claudius Hustons and Robert V. Lucases, whom he himself installed as the managers of its affairs.

He came in on the high tide of a prosperity which he claimed was wholly the act of the Republican Party. It was a golden era that under his ministrations would be broadened and deepened in its fruitfulness. He was the apostle of the New Economic Order, promising a chicken in every pot and two cars in every garage.

A year later millions were walking the streets out of work, Thousands of factories have been shut down. Thousands of concerns and businesses have gone into bankruptcy, and hundreds of banks have crashed and failed. Agricultural prices have sunk to the lowest levels in thirty years. Exports have fallen off hundreds of millions of dollars and throughout the length and breadth of the land there is want, hunger, despair, and tragedy.

When he entered the White House he was the hero of great humanitarian exploits. In Europe and Russia he had fed millions. He had never hesitated to come before Congress and ask for vast sums for this purpose.

When disaster overwhelmed millions of his own countrymen in the city and on the farm, he suddenly developed austere scruples. To feed the hungry by funds from the Federal Treasury was undesirable "charity" and a "dole." To do so by pitiful breadlines, by private and inadequate local charity, was not.

Violently and frantically he set his face against a Federal grant. While millions starved he talked of "self-reliance." And when finally he was compelled to give way and permit some relief, at least to drought-stricken farmers, he adamantly refused to allow the use of the word "food" and insisted upon "security" for the pittances reluctantly loaned them by the richest country in the world.

The three measures sponsored by Senator Wagner, of New York, projecting a sound program for dealing with depressions in the future, he secretly fought in the House of Representatives and when that chamber finally repudiated his leadership and enacted them, he vetoed the most vital, establishing a national employment exchange system.

His administration was to be one of great organizing and executive skill. He was the Great Engineer, the Great Executive. Confronted through depression, with one of the greatest opportunities in the history of the country for far-reaching social and economic reorganization, he completely blew up; and when a circus stunt, the so-called business conference he staged in the early days of the collapse, fell flat, he resorted to evasion, distorted statements and misrepresentations in a futile and hysterical effort to stem and belie the inexorable march of deflation.

His whole record throughout the great national disaster is

unbelievable for its abysmal incompetence, do-nothingness and reactionary stultification.

\*

WITHIN a year after he had taken office, the country was asking the question, "Why has Hoover failed?" There were few, not even among the staunchest members of his own party, who would not admit that he had failed to live up to expectations.

Such irreconcilable Hoovercrats as Senator Simeon D. Fess, fawning chairman of the Republican National Committee, and Will Irwin, his old classmate at Leland Stanford University, attributed his collapse to bad breaks, the drought, the stock crash, politics. But to the country at large the mystery of why a man apparently so preëminently qualified and so successfully advertised as the executive of executives should have so completely missed fire remained unsolved.

The answer is fourfold. The Hoover myth, the picture of the great engineer, qualified beyond all others to lead the Nation, was built up by one of the most skilful propaganda machines in the history of American politics.

Again, Hoover spent most of his life among the coolies of China and the wage-slaves of the Far East, where he reaped a great fortune and reputation through the exercise of the autocratic right of hire and fire. When he came to be the head of a great Democracy he found he could not fire a Senator who opposed him, unless he appointed him to an Ambassadorship, and there were only five of these to go around.

Third, when the fact dawned on him that the United States was a Democracy and he tried to play politics, he surrounded himself with politicians of the lowest order and who have made his Administration famous for its political ineptitude.

Lastly, and perhaps the most important answer to Herbert Hoover's failure is the fact that deeply ingrained in his make-up are two unfortunate characteristics, fear and vacillation, which, coupled with a petty personal temper, sorely try even his most loyal friends.

That Herbert Hoover was beset by this petty temper was not disclosed to any except those who knew him intimately until after he received the Republican nomination for President. Then with the spotlight of public curiosity focused upon him as never before, his fatal weaknesses of character began to come to light publicly.

As Secretary of Commerce he had, of course, been "in the news," in fact was the member of the Harding and Coolidge Cabinets who kept his name more consistently on the front pages than any other. But it was always in a secondary and impersonal rôle. When he stepped into the Presidential spotlight everything he did, said, or thought became public property. The spotlight of publicity dodged back and forth over every move he made, sought out every crevice of his private life, illuminated even his soul.

This was nothing new. It was the same with Coolidge. It was the same with Harding. It was the same with Wilson. It will be the same as long as the United States has a President and as long as the people of the United States insist upon treating their President as one of themselves rather than as Europe treats its monarchs.

Under these circumstances it is inevitable that sooner or later every fault and blemish, every whim and eccentricity of a man's life will be uncovered, particularly if he has such vital inadequacies as Herbert Hoover had to hide.

The first revelation of the Presidential temper came some weeks after Hoover had been nominated at Kansas City. He was living at Palo Alto, preparing for his acceptance speech. At the urgent requests of the newspaper photographers a morning was set aside for them to snap various "stills" and "movies" of the Hoovers at home.

Mrs. Hoover was self-appointed master of ceremonies. After all, it was her home and if it was going to be photographed, she wanted it done right. She ordered photographers over here, there and everywhere. She wanted chairs placed this way and benches that. Nothing seemed to please her. The photographers perspired and struggled. The newspapermen stood by amused. It was not their show. Mr. Hoover grew irritated. True he was sorely tried. Every one's sympathies were with him. And half a hundred people were watching him.

Finally, despite his audience, Mr. Hoover turned to his wife.

"You'd better run in the house now," he grumbled. "That will be all."

Mrs. Hoover looked a little startled. Then remembering how many people there were present, she smiled.

"All right," she replied cheerfully, and obeyed.

Another example of the Hoover temper was displayed on election night. Again he was in his home in Palo Alto. Election returns were being received and as the night went on and became apparent that he was the victor, neighbors and friends dropped in to congratulate him. In the course of the latter, some one laughingly remarked that the university vote showed a number of ballots for his opponent. Mr. Hoover immediately grew cold.

"I don't see how any intelligent person, especially a member of the Stanford faculty, could so misunderstand the issues of the campaign," he exclaimed indignantly, a dark scowl passing over his face.

A somewhat similar incident occurred when Mr. Hoover returned to his S Street home in Washington. One of his neighbors on S Street is Frederick A. Delano, prominent architect and once head of the opium commission to Persia. Mr. and Mrs. Delano are old friends of the Hoovers, and, after the latter's return to Washington, they called to pay their respects.

Tea was served. The conversation was vivacious. All went well until Fred Delano remarked:

"I must be quite frank with you, Mr. President. I voted for Al Smith. But now that you're elected, I'm extremely glad and I want to congratulate you."

Mr. Hoover did not reply. His conversation lagged. The coolness became so perceptible that the Delanos left within a few minutes.

Since entering the White House, Mr. Hoover has repeatedly revealed streaks of temper and pettiness.

One of his favorite pets was a massive police dog named "King Tut." The dog had the freedom of the White House grounds and frequently ran and walked with the President when the latter went back and forth between the residence and the executive offices.

One day the President on his way to lunch observed King Tut playing with one of the White House Guards. The President whistled. The dog looked up but did not come. Mr. Hoover whistled again. Still the dog remained with the guard. Mr. Hoover turned on his heel and went on.

That afternoon an order was issued that none of the White House staff should play with the White House pets.

Some time after this, the Baltimore *Sun* published an article reporting the fact that the bids for air mail contracts over certain western routes had been drawn up but were phrased in such a way that only one company could bid on them.

The article also called attention to the fact that Herbert Hoover, Jr. was employed with this firm.

At his next press conference, the President completely lost control of himself and denounced the article with a passion which few who know him have ever seen him display.

All these and many similar incidents, showing a streak of pettiness seldom before witnessed in the White House, contributed to the dissolution of the Hoover myth.

Even without them, however, the myth would have been dissolved. It rested on too artificial a foundation to stand the strain of the pitiless realities of the Presidency.

Every possible trick, every new device, known or capable of being invented by skilled publicity agents, had been invoked to make Hoover the Superman, the Great Executive, and a reputation thus made was all the more easily washed away.

How meticulous were not only Hoover's publicity experts but even he himself in building up this myth can be gauged from an incident which occurred in his office at the Department of Commerce. Mr. Hoover had been notified a few hours before that the Kansas City convention had nominated him for the Presidency and the photographers flocked in for a picture.

Mr. Hoover sat at his mahogany desk. No papers cluttered its shining surface. No mail remained to be answered. There was a silver inkwell, a row of push buttons. That was all. The stage was set for the filming of a picture of the Great Executive.

The cameramen took their first snap from a moderate distance, then picked up their tripods and swooped down for a close-up. The new nominee threw his hands in front of his face and fled from the room.

No close-ups for him! He knew his publicity game. He knew that in close-ups his face looked weak and flabby. It was not the face of the Great Executive, the Strong Man.

George Akerson, his secretary, inadvertently let this out while persuading the cameramen to retreat from the desk. Later he persuaded Mr. Hoover to return, and the cameramen took their pictures from a reasonable distance. What Mr. Hoover did not know, however, was that the cameramen during the confusion had put on their long distance lenses. They got their close-ups anyway.

Before he became President, Mr. Hoover got so in the habit of getting across his publicity in a big way, so accustomed to having the public believe, without challenging it, whatever he had to say, that it was the most natural thing in the world for him to believe he could continue to do this after he entered the White House.

He started out with his memorable announcement that the Presidential yacht, the Mayflower, would be scrapped. He explained that he took this step because the ship was too expensive and also because the men who manned her were needed in the service. Immediately after, he took not only the eighty marines who served on the Mayflower—and who were needed in the service—but twice that number to build his Rapidan fishing camp, and later had a company of army engineers from Fort Humphreys sent in to build roads for the place.

Again there was his memorable statement of 1929 that he was going to pare army costs. It brought him loud cheers from almost the entire press and the general public. But when some months later the budget was submitted to Congress, it was found that army costs had not been reduced. Few people knew this, however, and all in all, the statement got just what it was calculated to get—a generous amount of good Presidential publicity.

Most of Mr. Hoover's statements during the London naval negotiations were on the same order. He started out with the glamorous announcement that the United States would hold up the building of three cruisers. He followed it with a statement trying to prove that the results of the London Conference had been real reduction, when, as a matter of fact, the London Treaty fixed the total construction program at a figure higher than ever before.

By this time, however, the press in general and Congress in particular had become suspicious of his high-sounding words and had begun to inquire for themselves just what the facts were. In the case of the alleged suspended cruisers, reporters for the New York *Evening Post* and the New York *Sun* discovered that no orders had gone out to the Navy Department to stop work on them, but, on the contrary, all preparation for the construction of the vessels was going forward as per schedule.

His statements summing up the work of the London Naval Conference, in which he undertook to make the upward limitation agreement appear as a momentous reduction achievement, aroused widespread protest. He undertook to set up the wholly false comparison of the extreme big-navy figures of the unsuccessful Geneva Naval Conference, held three years previous, with the lesser tonnage of the London Treaty.

So completely untenable was this claim that it was never once adverted to by Administration spokesmen throughout the long committee hearings and the Senate debate on the pact.

At the beginning of the last session of the Seventy-first Congress, the President announced that the Treasury deficit would be about $185,000,000. A week later, when the Budget was published, it disclosed that actually the deficit was estimated as likely to be more than $500,000,000.

The time between the President's announcement and publication of the official estimate was so short that one of two conclusions was unavoidable: either Mr. Hoover was woefully ignorant of the fiscal affairs of the Government or was playing politics with figures.

As a result of these and many other such misrepresentations, every statement the President now makes is minutely scrutinized. As Secretary of Commerce he was accustomed to having his word accepted as gospel. The oracle spoke; every one listened. As President, his statements have attained such an unsavory reputation for being purely inspired, purely unfounded publicity blasts, that whenever he proclaims business to be picking up, the stock market goes down.

So regularly has this occurred that in September, 1930, when construction activities in the United States showed an upturn for the first time in many months, the Treasury Department advised the White House not to announce it for fear of an unfavorable repercussion on the stock market.

Despite the sweeping and unfounded statements he is in the habit of making in his own defense, the President is not only super-sensitive but literally quails and becomes hysterical when he himself is attacked.

Members of President Wilson's White House staff relate that during the War any unfriendly remark made in Congress about Mr. Hoover was sure to mean a visit from him. He would complain bitterly to Mr. Wilson and frequently threatened to resign unless protected from such congressional outbursts.

During the Coolidge Administration, when Henry C. Wallace was Secretary of Agriculture, Mr. Hoover once complained to Coolidge that Wallace's farm journal was attacking him. Coolidge, however, looked bored. He told his Secretary of Commerce about his own discovery—that it was much more comfortable not to read "things that are agin' you."

How Mr. Hoover came to build his political reputation on the shifting and uncertain sands of a propaganda machine is easy to understand. He had been doing this all his life.

The secret of his success as an engineer was promotion. Actually his work was not engineering. At the height of his business career he was receiving $5,000 a year as "mining expert," and $95,000 a year as a "financial expert."

His job was to promote, to organize and then pass on. In all that vast area which he ranged, from Siberia to Australia and from China to Africa, there is to be found to-day not a single engineering project which bears his name and the stamp of his handiwork. Of concessions with which he was connected, however, there are many.

When he retired from "engineering" he did so to become the organizer of his own concession-holding ventures in foreign lands. From an office in London he promoted a long list of mining enterprises, listed by the British Mining Manual of 1912 as the Burma Mines, Ltd., Inter-Argentina Syndicate, Ltd., Inter-Russian Syndicate, Ltd., Russo-Asiatic Corporation, Ltd., Yuanmi Gold Mines, Ltd., Babilonia Gold Mines, Ltd.

It was as a thirteen-year-old youngster in Oregon that Herbert Hoover first learned to become a promoter. He was associated with his uncle in jobbing off now relatively worthless real estate in Salem, Oregon, during one of those "California-Florida" land booms which are always promising an Eldorado to the American people. His uncle's company was out to sell land. It found it was losing sales to rival companies. Young Herbert conceived the idea of meeting newcomers at the station, settling them in private boarding houses, thus giving his uncle's salesmen an opportunity to talk to them without competition.

With the commission young Herbert got from renting the rooms, he helped finance himself through college. From that time on, he never ceased promoting.

*

IT is not difficult to understand why Herbert Hoover has played politics ineptly, why he does not get along with people, and why he has surrounded himself with yes-men.

All of that period of his life during which a man's character and mental process are molded was spent far from the field of politics in isolated parts of the world. Months and years spent on the edge of the Australian desert or in the interior of China rob any man of that contact with his fellowmen so essential if he is to inspire leadership. Especially true is this when the people with whom he is surrounded on the edge of that desert or in the interior of China remain there subject to his whim and pleasure.

It was in these circumstances that Herbert Hoover developed the habits of autocracy which have so handicapped him in the White House. Because he had the power to command, he never developed the power to lead. His word was law. Once, expounding his views on labor troubles to a friend, he told how he had always found that chaining a Chinese coolie to a stake for a day in the hot sun was conducive to good discipline and a minimum of strikes.

How ruthless was Herbert Hoover's business conduct in China has been told in the High Court of Justice, Chancery Division, London, in the suit brought against his firm in 1905 by Chang Yen Mao, Director-General of mines for the Chinese Government. Chang accused Hoover and his associates of euchring him out of some valuable mining property, and Mr. Justice Joyce in rendering the decision against Hoover and his company said:

> "Incidentally it appears by a letter of Mr. Hoover that he actually took possession of some title deeds of the property by main force. Under the circumstances, I am of opinion that to

allow the defendant company, while they insist on retaining the benefits of the transfer, to escape from the obligations of the memorandum upon any such pretext as that Hoover or De-Wouters were not authorized to agree to its terms, or that it was impossible for the defendant company to perform some of these terms without altering its constitution, would be contrary to one of the plainest principles of equity. It would be to sanction such a flagrant breach of faith as, in my opinion, could not be tolerated by the law of any country."

And in conclusion, the Judge added these significant words:

"I think," he said, "that I ought to make one more observation, which is that, in the investigation taken before me of the transaction in question, it has not been shown to me that His Excellency Chang has been guilty of any breach of faith or of any impropriety at all, which is more than I can say for some of the other parties concerned."

A man cannot spend some twenty years of his life experiencing this unnatural relation toward his fellow-men without becoming permanently influenced by it, without becoming dictatorial, autocratic and a perpetual dependent upon the right of "hire and fire."

The result is that Mr. Hoover, both as Secretary of Commerce and as President, constantly has surrounded himself with inferiors, men who accept his word without challenge and carry it out.

When thrown in contact with equals, with men whom he could not discharge, he has failed abysmally. This factor is perhaps the greatest reason for the political turmoil which has attended every month of his administration.

Finding that he could not "fire" a Senator or a Representative, the President has alternated between abject surrender and weak, stupid bluffing, in which he has never yet been successful.

Early in his administration, Representative Bertram Snell, hard-boiled Chairman of the House Rules Committee, returned from a conference with the President regarding the latter's attempt to take control of New York State patronage and ribaldly reassured his colleagues.

"I have met the President and he is ours," Snell announced.

There is not a really significant Republican leader in Congress or the country at large who trusts or respects Mr. Hoover. Some of his bitterest critics are to be found among Republican Senate and House leaders who have confidential relations with him.

During the Arkansas food-relief controversy in the closing days of the Seventy-first Congress, Republican leaders refused to assume the responsibility of assuring the Democrats that the proceeds of the compromise $20,000,000 appropriation would be used for "human" relief as well as "animal" relief. Senator McNary, who had been double-crossed by the White House on the same issue at the beginning of the session, bluntly sent word to the President that he was through pledging his word for him and that if the President had any promises to make he would have to make them himself.

It was also during the course of the two months' struggle over the food-relief issue that there occurred the astounding spectacle of the President issuing a statement defending his policy and attacking the opposition, and when they turned on him and lashed him mercilessly, for a week straight, not one responsible Republican leader in the entire country rose to say a word in his behalf.

Most of Mr. Hoover's administration has been a series of surrenders to one political faction after another.

He has been cowed by petty state and local politicians into making appointments he was against. In Pennsylvania they bullied him into naming Albert L. Watson and, in Kansas, Richard J. Hopkins to Federal judgeships, despite the fact that his Attorney General pronounced both unfit for the Federal bench.

The Old Guard high-tariff gang cowed him into signing the Smoot-Hawley Tariff Act which in a thousand ways violated every view he had ever held on the tariff and which, up to a few hours before he furtively announced his approval, he had described to his friends as vicious, extortionate and obnoxious.

Even the Insurgents, whom he hates, on more than one occasion have forced the President to bow to their demands. Threatening a fight on confirmation, they forced him to withdraw the name of Lieutenant General Edgar Jadwin as Chairman of the Federal Power Commission, and, by defeating a fifth-rate appointment he attempted to foist upon the Supreme Court, compelled him to name Justice Owen J. Roberts, a man of outstanding ability.

So abject and tortuous has been the President's course, that even such slavish Republican newspapers as the Chicago *Tribune,* the New York *Evening Post* and the New York *Herald Tribune* have denounced and berated him with bitter indignation.

Elected on a platform of taking important appointments out of politics, Mr. Hoover has played politics with almost every appointment he has made.

Instead of merit, ability and character, political expediency alone has counted with him. His record in judicial appointments is unsurpassed for mediocrity and partisanship. As Minister to Canada, he sent a blatant super-patriot known among his fellow-service men as "Boob" McNider. As Ambassador to Berlin, he sent Senator Frederic M. Sackett, a machine politician who dared not face a reëlection contest in Kentucky. As Ambassador to France, he sent Senator Walter E. Edge, whose ownership of the Dorland Advertising Agency, vigorous competitor of the French official agency, somewhat embarrassed Franco-American relations.

A vacancy on the Supreme Court of the United States he attempted to use to strengthen a collapsing political machine in the South, and the International Joint Commission, which he had declared he would reorganize to carry out important American-Canadian negotiations, he has completely debased by packing it with decrepit lame-duck Senators and an un-wanted Post Office official.

Afforded an exceptional opportunity to strengthen the government's regulation of the great water-power industry through the creation by Congress of the new Federal Power Commission, he ransacked the land for unknown and ame-nable mediocrities and appointed them to the Commission. Of all the outstanding experts and authorities that he could have obtained he picked these five wholly inexperienced and unin-formed nonentities and turned this vital responsibility over to them.

Not only did he surround himself with one of the most mediocre, and most servile Cabinets in history, but during the first two years of his incumbency, he appointed three National Republican Committee Chairmen: Hubert M. Work, a blun-derer; Claudius Huston, a lobbyist; and Simeon D. Fess, an Anti-Saloon League-ridden and reactionary Senator.

While Mr. Hoover has some precedent for playing politics with this type of appointment, there has been no President in recent history who has reached into the departments of his Cabinet officers and dictated the appointment of their as-sistants.

Mr. Hoover has done this repeatedly, the two most glaring instances being the appointment of William R. Castle, Jr., as Under Secretary of State, and of General Douglas Mac-Arthur as Chief of Staff. Secretary Stimson, in the case of Castle, and Secretary Hurley, in the case of MacArthur, both vigorously opposed the appointments, and yet despite the fact that the success of their departments depends upon harmony with their chief assistants, Mr. Hoover insisted that these men be named.

No instance of the petty political prejudice of the President has been more revealing, however, than that of his veto of the Wagner Bill, proposing the establishment of a national employment exchange system.

The veto affords a profoundly illuminating insight into the

character of Herbert Hoover. It was inspired purely by personal and political dislike of the sponsor of the bill, Senator Wagner, a Tammany Democrat and an intimate friend of Alfred E. Smith.

In 1920-'21-'23-'24 Mr. Hoover specifically and categorically associated himself with recommendations for the establishment of exactly such an employment bureau system as Senator Wagner proposed.

In 1920, as Chairman of President Wilson's Industrial Conference, Mr. Hoover recommended "enactment of appropriate legislation by Congress making provision for an employment clearing house under Federal control." In 1921, as Chairman of President Harding's Conference on Unemployment, he recommended an "adequate permanent system of employment offices." In 1923 as Secretary of Commerce, he appointed a committee on business cycles which recommended "a national system of employment bureaus." In 1924 he appointed a Committee on Seasonal Operations which endorsed the previous recommendations.

He rejected the Wagner Bill, despite the repeated pleas of Colonel Arthur Woods, Chairman of his Unemployment Committee, that it be approved. He did so on the ground that the bill would abolish an already existing system that the year before had found jobs for 1,300,000 workers. That both statements were false was proven by the fact that exactly six weeks after he had killed the bill, he became alarmed at the growing volume of denunciation of his action, and undertook to set up, by Executive order, very much the same system.

The Wagner Bill specifically provided that the existing United States Employment Service should not be displaced until the new and more desirable system was in operation. Furthermore, the old Federal service had not found work for 1,300,000 applicants in 1930.

It had placed 700,000 seasonal workers, of the harvest hand type. In this field the problem is not finding jobs but workers who will take them. In the fields where the difficulty is finding employment, such as in industry, business, and offices, the Federal agency accomplished practically nothing.

The 1,300,000 that the President claimed for it was a deliberate misrepresentation. Six hundred thousand of these jobs were actually found by State Employment Bureaus whose only connection with the Federal system was through the designation of one of their staff as a Federal Employment Supervisor, for which he received $1 a year.

Of the same character was the President's refusal to permit Senator Wagner to be chairman of a special committee the Senate authorized on his motion to inquire into unemployment insurance measures. It is an unwritten Senate rule that the sponsor of a special committee is always named its chairman. In recognition of this precedent Vice President Curtis appointed Wagner as the first man on the committee, thus confirming his right to the chairmanship. But when Wagner, and the two Old Guard Senators named as his associates, met to organize the committee, they shamefacedly informed him that the President was opposed to his being chairman and they would have to unseat him. Being docile party hacks they proceeded to carry out their instructions, thus robbing Wagner of the opportunity of doing the constructive work he had planned.

*

WHEN Herbert Hoover was a small boy in Iowa, his father operated a barbed-wire factory, and, anxious to improve his product, he hit upon the idea of covering the steel strands with tar.

One day young Bertie, standing beside the steaming caldron of tar and wondering whether it would burn, tossed a flaming stick into it. The conflagration which resulted destroyed his father's plant and nearly wiped out the little town and his father's store.

"That night," according to Rose Wilder Lane, one of Hoover's most adulatory biographers, "he heard his father tell how the store, and perhaps the town had been saved. The fire, it was thought, had been caused by the unwatched kettle of tar, which must have boiled over. Bertie said nothing. If he had been asked, he would have told what he had done, but no one asked him.

"He sat unnoticed, eating silently. He was sorry and terrified, yet he was glad. It was such a strange feeling that when he had gone to bed he lay awake for a long time, hearing the katydid in the wild crab-apple tree outside his window. He had done a frightening thing; the shock of it was still in his nerves and the crime of it on his conscience, but he had not meant to do wrong. He had been innocently experimenting, and the result was not entirely disheartening.

" 'Anyway, I found out what it would do,' he thought. 'I found it out all by myself.' He wondered if he would be punished if he told. He thought not. But he decided that it was best to keep his own counsel in the matter.

"And for forty years he did so."

The story is one of the most revealing incidents in Herbert Hoover's life. It gives the key to many qualities in his character which both his friends and his enemies have been trying to explain.

It explains his vacillation, his indecision, the worry through which he passes before making up his mind. It explains his hesitancy in facing issues, a hesitancy which sometimes borders on outright cowardice. It explains why he privately denounced the oil scandals of the Harding Administration and yet sat unmoved throughout that régime, never denouncing it publicly. It explains why he hesitated three days before accepting the rôle of Belgian Food Administrator which the Allies had offered him. It explains his basic intellectual timidity, his inability to grapple in a straightforward and forthright manner with vital issues, why he is always resorting to such indirect devices as commissions to relieve him of the responsibility of acting on controversial questions.

It explains also why on such a moot question as prohibition, he has never once said one word that positively and definitely stated whether he is wet or dry. Senator Carter Glass of Virginia once offered to pay $1,000 to any one who could produce a single categorical dry declaration by the President. Several years have passed since then but no one has ever claimed the reward.

From his "noble experiment" reply to Senator Borah, in the pre-nomination campaign in 1928, to this day the President has never made a positive statement of his stand, either for or against prohibition. Throughout his campaign he lurked behind the screen of enforcement, while his managers and spokesmen gave assurances to both sides, representing him dry to the drys and wet to the wets.

From this policy he has never deviated. Every dry-by-implication statement he has made has been followed immediately by an under-cover wet "interpretation." This occurred when he gave out his pronouncement on the Wickersham Commission Prohibition Report and after his acceptance speech, at Palo Alto, California, in the summer of 1928.

In that address his remarks regarding prohibition were widely accepted as meaning he was dry. The next day, a close friend, who had worked with him in the drafting of the address, called in reporters representing wet newspapers, and solely for "local consumption" gave them a wet "slant" on the President's remarks. These papers used this interpretation in his behalf throughout his Presidential campaign.

The day following his expression on the Wickersham Report select correspondents were called to the White House and there given a distinct wet interpretation of the declaration.

On the power issue the President's course has been even more tortuous and reactionary. He is wedded to private, monopolistic ownership and control of this great and vital industry. Yet, during the whole of his 1928 Presidential campaign he was grimly silent on this major problem—with one local exception.

When he spoke at Elizabethton, Tennessee, he made a veiled reference to government operation under certain conditions. Muscle Shoals is a matter of greatest moment to this section.

The editor of a nearby Scripps-Howard newspaper, speaking to him privately, asked him if he had Muscle Shoals in mind as one of these exceptions.

"You may say that means Muscle Shoals," the President told him. The Scripps-Howard papers, supporting him, published it widely.

Press associations and newspapermen, upon his return to his campaign headquarters in Washington, inquired as to the accuracy of the story. After several hours of conferences with political and campaign advisors, the President issued a statement in which he declared that "there is no question of government ownership (of Muscle Shoals) as the government already owns both the power and nitrate plants."

Not a word was to be found in the statement about government operation, which was the question raised, and not ownership. The tenor and implication of the statement, however, indicated approval of government operation of Muscle Shoals. The message was so accepted by the public and the press and not denied by Hoover.

Yet, from then on, he covertly fought and opposed every effort to enact a sound government-operation program for the great plant. Through his control of the House of the Seventy-first Congress he obstructed and sabotaged such legislation as long as he could, and when, finally, after months of laborious negotiation, powerfully assisted by the defeat for reëlection of his spokesman in the House on the question, an acceptable measure was enacted, he vetoed it in a message filled with misstatements and misrepresentations.

His course on governmental regulation of utilities has been equally devious.

Addressing the annual convention in 1925 of the National Electric Light Association, the trade organization of the utility industry, he insisted that there had been outrageous exaggeration concerning the need for control of public utilities. Such supervision in "purely local affairs," he contended, would prove a menace to individual initiative.

This anti-Federal regulation pronouncement in 1925 was a reversal of views he expressed when he addressed the Association Conventions in 1922 and 1924. Then he saw a hopeful rôle for the national government in coördinating and strengthening the regulations of power developments that were outside he jurisdiction of the individual states.

etween his 1925 speech and 1929, he maintained a tight on the question of regulation. Not even his Presiden- could force him to speak out on so important a ing any other information, it was generally taken uring these years that his views were unchanged s against Federal regulation.

essage to Congress in 1929, he again turned a is time going back to his more liberal ideas 24. He conceded that there were instances of aracter that were beyond the control of the states ended to Congress that it extend the authority of Power Commission.

 reversed his reversal, the President promptly is policy once again. This time he did it covertly and irection.

hrough a member of his Cabinet he attacked the idea of Federal regulation while personally, by means of weak appointments, he stultified the effectiveness of the Federal Power Commission, whose creation he had recommended to Congress for the purpose of strengthening governmental control.

Secretary of Interior Wilbur, President-on-leave of Leland Stanford University, which has large water power investments, attacked Federal regulation in the last annual report of the old Federal Power Commission, of which he was the dominant member, and advocated state supervision as the sound and wise way to deal with this stupendous problem.

Attorney General Mitchell coöperated in this undercover drive by rendering an astounding legal opinion in which he undertook by interpretation to repeal practically every portion of the Federal Water Power Act set up by Congress over two decades ago for the protection of the public.

This amazing attack on a statute he was sworn to safeguard and defend by the highest legal representative of the government raised such a storm of protest that the old Power Commission did not dare proceed on it as Wilbur had intended.

Judge George W. Woodruff, Solicitor for the Department of Interior under President Roosevelt and one of the authors of the Water Power Act, declared that if the opinion were allowed to go unchallenged it would sweep away years of effort to protect the interests of the future generations in vast water power rights.

"The public stewards," he said, "become the exploiters of public property. The crisis is very grave."

President Hoover never repudiated or made any statement regarding either Wilbur's or Mitchell's action.

\*

IN the long and tragic travail of the economic depression the most tragic thing was the President's fear of admitting that a great disaster had befallen the country. For months, while gloom, unemployment, and deflation settled on the land, he refused to admit their reality or do anything fundamental about the situation. His approach to the problem was wholly that of the boomer, the bull-market operator, concerned only with his own political interests and willing to resort to any device or misrepresentation to further them.

Facts, statistics, plan, organization—there have been none, and when proposed by others have been rejected and stifled, secretly when possible, openly when that was impossible.

One policy alone has dominated his course: not to do or say anything that would reveal the truth about the great catastrophe. Suppression and inaction have been his unshaken rule.

The detailed record of this effort tells the story eloquently:

the most intellectually dishonest statements ever to come from the White House."

The final story of Herbert Hoover is yet to be told. Only time will make available the mass of secret documents and the details of his business career, now so zealously guarded, by which the complete picture can be filled in. Only time also will tell the final story of how Herbert Hoover was pushed into a plan to postpone German reparations and Allied debt payments; a plan which Owen D. Young had worked out and which Henry L. Stimson, coöperating with the British government, had urged upon his chief in the White House; a plan which was finally put over on Herbert Hoover through the combined efforts of Charles G. Dawes, Dwight W. Morrow and Andrew W. Mellon plus a dozen New York bankers who clamored at him in person and by long distance telephone for nearly a month. Finally, his confidence restored by a trip to the hospitable Middle West, Mr. Hoover adopted the plan and was never more surprised in his life when it was heralded as his master stroke.

Whether it will carry him on to reëlection, only time can tell. But time long after that will tell the story of one of the super-promoters of the age.

It will be the story of a paradox. A man who, despite the handicap of a fundamental timorousness, was able by a consummate sense of publicity to create the illusion of heroism and greatness and to attain for a time world acclaim.

It will be the story of a man who had the genius to create a great rôle, but lacked the essential requisites of character to enact it. It will be the story of a success which failed because it succeeded too well.

Had Herbert Hoover never gained the Presidency, he might well have remained a shimmering hero. The illusion he so skilfully wove never would have been shattered. But before the ruthless realities and the merciless tests of that office his fundamental inadequacy of character undid him and he stands to-day stripped of all his carefully conjured glories.

## CHAPTER FOUR

## EGG CHARLEY

*F*OR a third of a century, in the House and in the Senate, Charley Curtis, of Kansas, drew his salary and mileage, spread abroad in unrestrained generosity the garden seeds and moral documents paid for by the Treasury, planted his share of patronage where it served him best, upheld loyally the hand of the President—if he was a Republican—and in all other ways was a steady, dependable, unquestioning Party plug, dull, regular, and conforming, no worse than the rest of the pack and in some ways a lot better.

By political standards, he was a pretty square shooter. He didn't pose as a sage or a superman; he didn't steal; he never went Red hunting; and if he waved the flag and occasionally declaimed sonorously about home and mother he was at least not of the smug type of Senator David Reed of Pennsylvania, the Mellon political and legal bodyguard, nor of the buffoon ilk of Senator Tom Heflin.

Coming from Kansas, he was a voting dry, of course. But he made no secret of the fact that he was fond of a good game of draw poker, and nothing gave him greater pleasure than to take a $1.25 pot from Senator "Jim" Couzens of Michigan, who, despite his $40,000,000 Ford-made fortune, would always howl in anguish.

Charley didn't profess to be a regular church-goer. His

skill in profanity was widely recognized and he was an enthusiastic and regular patron of the ponies.

Of course, no one ever accused him of being a Progressive. But the feminists, nevertheless, called him friend, and it is one of the proudest of his claims that he led the Senate fight for the Nineteenth Amendment and was the author of a bill protecting the rights of American women sufficiently affluent to hire foreigners to marry them and of another creating a series of select Federal women's prisons for ladies tangled up with the law. Finally, his vote was recorded for the Child Labor Amendment—and whether the fact that Kansas has no mills had anything to do with it is perhaps beside the question.

In those carefree congressional days Charley liked nothing better than to chin with the boys in mocking manner about the social game in Washington, about which he troubled himself not at all and in which he felt like a fish out of water. The pushing and climbing of some of his colleagues and of the other strutters in the official arena were a source of much amusement to him, and his comments thereon were tart and devastating.

Altogether, he was personally a decent enough fellow—for an Old Guard Senator.

He played the political game in a smooth, efficient manner, and not too offensively, and thus for thirty-three years he served Kansas and the Republican Party. He made no speeches if he could help it, and when, in the closing years of his congressional career, he became Republican floor leader of the Senate and would rise from his seat and bring endless hours of hokum to a close with "Mr. President, I move we adjourn," his name was called blessed by all.

This daily motion was his sole contribution to statecraft during his years as majority leader. His name is not written on any legislation of importance, either good or bad, but who is there who will not grant that Charley also served?

But while on the surface he was always a placid, humble,

unchanging, decent fellow, his long years in Washington finally left their mark on him.

In his old age he was stricken with soaring ambitions and they began to plague him. His humility turned to gall.

A life-long inferiority complex, arising out of his Kaw Indian descent, began to be complicated by the recurrence of a childhood fairy story that every American may hope to be President.

This fixation took hold of him as his physical powers declined, and in a short time it had flamed into an irrepressible libido.

The idea of aspiring to the Presidency came to him quite suddenly. Mediocrity in the Presidency had become the fashion and he was not only mediocrity incarnate, but, as politicians go, more or less honest—a combination far from common, and one, just then, urgently needed by the Republican Party.

If Harding and Coolidge could reach for the purple, why not he?

He was not—at least, not then—a man given to thumping his chest in self-righteousness, but his comfortable little paunch and his soft, round, copper-brown jowls covered a dogged heart and a determined jaw. Once the fatal aspiration to imperial grandeur was implanted in his psyche, it possessed him completely.

The idea of a Red man, even though only a half-breed, sitting in the White House made him sweat and pant with wonder and delight. He saw himself in the stirring rôle of uplifter of a broken race. And in no time at all there were plenty of sycophants about him to help the idea along.

It didn't take Charley long to get started and once under way the illusion grew by leaps and bounds. A first-hand knowledge of the putrid deal that resulted in Harding's nomination and an intimate acquaintance with what took place during the several years of his Presidency enormously strengthened Charley's determination to run.

When, in 1924, some one proposed that he be made Cool-

idge's running-mate, the new complex burst into full and fiery
bloom. He became a definite candidate—first for the Presidency, and then, if that turned out to be impossible, for the
noble desuetude of Vice President. Coolidge's petulant rejection
of his name, because Charley had opposed him, as had most
of the other Republican Senators, on the Soldiers' Bonus hand-
out, only increased the pressure in his gauges.

In a quiet, skilful way he set about restoring himself in the
favor of the White House. When, after the 1924 election, it
became apparent that Coolidge and Dawes loved each other
like a pair of strange cats, Charley utilized to the full the
advantage the place as Senate floor leader gave him and set
about making himself solid. No painted warrior on the trail
ever trod a more wary and skilful path than he in the puerile
wrangling between the Senate and the little Yankee carpet-
bagger.

When the Equalization Fee fight was on he voted for both
the bill itself and to sustain Coolidge's veto of it, all the time
braying into the skies about the trials and burdens of the
befuddled farmer.

When, early in 1927, he became ill, he brooded darkly over
the possibility that death might intervene between him and
his goal. He doctored grimly, and despite the call of a trying
legislative situation, dropped everything and hustled off to
Florida to nurse himself back to health.

From then on he adhered carefully to a strict regimen,
taking long walks, eating with caution, and abandoning all-
night poker sessions.

All this time Charley was still keeping within the bounds
of reason. The Presidency he thought of only as a wistful
possibility. His real and immediate goal was the Vice Presidency.

But when Coolidge outsmarted himself with his famous "I
do not choose to run" statement and the bewildered Republican zealots took his words for what they appeared to say and

the race for the 1928 nomination was thrown open, Charley's final efflorescence rapidly set in.

One by one such appalling candidates as Jim Watson, Willis of Ohio, and the egregious Goff solemnly strutted forward and set up their claims. It is not, therefore, to be wondered at that Charley, observing their gall, suddenly ran amok—and promptly passed from reality altogether.

His madness, to be sure, was not altogether without its logic. With Coolidge out, and such men as Watson, Willis, and Goff accepted as serious contenders, he reasoned, there was a real chance for him, too.

Wasn't there every likelihood that history would repeat itself? Might not the leaders, Hoover, Lowden, Dawes, kill one another off and deadlock?

And might not the oil and high tariff bosses, turning to the second-stringers, cast their eyes upon the Indian Brave from Kansas?

Was he not from the Corn Belt, supposedly deeply disaffected? Wasn't he a friend of the farmer, and yet a party man of unimpeachable regularity and conservatism?

And finally, wasn't there a chance that, if the worst came to the worst, a good strong grab for the Presidency would make him a sure shot for second place.

Thus he reasoned—at first. But as the fight developed, ambition soared and raged within him. His walk may be the waddle of a fat old squaw, but brave warrior blood of the Red man of the plains courses in his veins.

Charley, in the hectic days of the spring of '28, actually came to believe that he would be President. Watson, Goff and Dawes might secretly consider themselves outside long-shots, but not Charley. He knew that he was a man of destiny.

So Charley set about to hack, hammer and wangle his way to the White House. He wrote thousands of letters enthusiastically extolling his virtues and proclaiming his availability. He opened headquarters in various States. He formally joined the anti-Hoover forces and metamorphosed a casual contempt for his opponent into a bitter Indian-like hatred.

To nominate Hoover, he said, publicly and privately, would be to place a hopeless burden upon an already overladen party. Hoover was intolerable, unspeakable, unthinkable.

That Hoover finally beat him he has never forgiven—and never will now that every day of Hoover's administration brings further proof to Charley that everything he said about him in the nomination campaign has been more than realized since he took office.

To this day Charley believes that he was double-crossed on the nomination. Those who know him well say he is sure that if Mellon and the Pennsylvania gang had played him square he would be in the White House to-day. They assert that he had promises from the Pennsylvania bosses, who distrusted Hoover, that he would get their backing.

Indeed, if they had gone over to him at the right moment at Kansas City, he might well have been chosen. Stranger things have happened at Republican conventions

Many reasons give Charley cause to believe that way. To begin with, Hoover was a minority candidate when the delegates assembled at the convention. Outside of the paid Negro cohorts from the South, carefully garnered by the sly C. Bascom Slemp and the mysterious Claudius Huston, and closely guarded after a Lowden kidnapping raid the day before the convention opened, he had only a few States actually pledged to him.

New York, dominated by Charles D. Hilles, and Pennsylvania, presumably controlled by Mellon and Joseph R. Grundy, wanted Coolidge, or anybody but Hoover. Lowden was obviously out of it. Thus, if these two big Eastern delegations had been thrown to Charley, as he was assured they would be, they might very well have swung the anti-Hoover majority to him.

Then, after a few ballots with Hoover losing ground,

Charley would have captured the rail on the home stretch and clattered in the winner.

But Coolidge's duplicity left his henchmen, William M. Butler, of Massachusetts, Hilles, and Mellon, completely up in the air—his autobiographical explanations, to the contrary notwithstanding. Thus a situation arose which the Hoover organization was quick to take full advantage of, with its powerful propaganda machine, servile press support and limitless financial resources.

The mass of delegates, standing around open-mouthed, waited for a push in some direction. William S. Vare (Philadelphia boss), with a hopeful eye to the Senate contest over his disputed seat and to the chance of giving the greatest Secretary of the Treasury since Hamilton a good swift boot, put over a fast one and came out for Hoover. Mellon and his muscle-man, Senator David Reed, bewildered and groggy over Vare's lightning play, found themselves trotting dejectedly with the Hoover herd.

The rest was simple—to Charley's heart-rending anguish.

His outburst the day before the convention, in which he had fervently declared that Hoover could not be nominated because "we don't want a candidate we will have to apologize for," while commendably frank, almost lost him the Vice Presidency.

In fact, if Coolidge had not put over a final bluff on the Hoover crowd, in a message to the effect that if Dawes, whom they really wanted, was nominated, he would consider it a personal affront, Charley, instead of being where he can give full play to his grandeur libido would be a sad and disillusioned Indian to-day.

With Dawes out, there was no one else at the moment, and so he got the break, thanks to Borah.

Goff and Watson, the Hoover people would not stand for. Fuller of Massachusetts dripped too freshly with Sacco-Vanzetti gore. Teddy Roosevelt, Jr., and Representative Tilson,

House leader, who panted and groveled for the place, couldn't even muster their own delegations.

So, after a night of futile searching, conferring and dickering, made notable by the pursuit by the reporters of blundering old "Doc" Hubert Work, Hoover's Campaign Manager, as he tried to sneak up and down the stairs of the Muehlbach Hotel in an effort to evade them, Hoover and the convention bosses threw up their hands and turned to Charley—as a last resort.

Next morning Borah piously mounted the rostrum and nominated him, to a pathetic scattering of applause.

And then Charley, like the true party wheel-horse that he is, swallowed his bitter words of a day or so before, and began the bleat he mouthed so dolorously all through the campaign: "And now I want to tell you about a man whose heart beats for the woman and the child, a man who, blah, blah, blah... Herbert Hoover... I thank you."

But in realization came also frustration and therein is to be found the clew to the strange mood that came over Charley when he assumed the Vice Presidency.

Believing, as he does, that but for a foul deal of fate he might have been nominated President, and that even to-day there stands between him and his consuming ambition only a fat, harried, and miserably inadequate man, Charley in his heart of hearts always sees himself in the White House.

In his improved raiment, his measured whispering, his determined reserve, his rabid clamor for full official honors upon any and all occasions, he has but one thought—the Presidency.

That is the secret of Charley as he is to-day. If the White House portals should ever actually open to him, he would be the most presidential President in the history of the land.

As has already been indicated, Charley is really a pleasant, homey enough sort of fellow. The world has guffawed at his outcries in defense of his deep-bosomed sister-hostess' social status, but little it knows the high ideals and lofty sentiments that prompted this hazardous crusade.

First of all, there is Sister Dolly herself—no small item.

Sister Dolly is a most determined and ambitious lady. By blood a half-sister—the Indian half missing—she, too, like Charley, has risen from the lowliest beginnings.

The wash tub and the kitchen range are not unknown to Dolly. The delicate nuances of society are of little moment to her. What Dolly wants she wants, and with Brother Charley as Vice President the esoteric superiorities of Senate ladies, Cabinet ladies, and Diplomatic dames awe her not at all.

Dolly, well over two hundred pounds and arrayed like Solomon when in all his kingly glory, is determined to have her rightful place and there is no squeamishness about her as to how she gets it.

And if she and Charley should by chance ever take up residence at 1600 Pennsylvania Avenue, with what relish would they both pay off scores! Many a society matron would pay dearly for the cutting jibes and smarting flippancies they now so gayly hurl at the pair.

There lopes about Washington a story that Charley's Indian name, literally translated, means Man-afraid-of-his-sister. No doubt that is wholly apocryphal, but what is true is that there is a real and strong bond of affection between brother and half-sister. Some years ago, when Mrs. Curtis was a helpless invalid, Dolly voluntarily took up the care and management of Charley's household, and this kindness over trying years has naturally not lessened his affection for her.

But it is not alone brotherly love and gratitude that inspired Charley to make his crusade for a due and proper recognition of the eminence, importance and dignity of the Vice Presidency. Deeper and profounder motives set him off.

No one knew better than he how useless and utterly ornamental the office really is. His years in the Senate and as a floor leader had left him no doubt on that score.

Also, as a Senator and floor leader, he had countenanced no change of the Vice President's lowly status. But once in the rôle himself, he saw things in a different light.

As Vice President, Charley approached the office from the angle of his Presidential fixation.

The Vice Presidency at best is a gamble. Its incumbents live only to fill a dead man's place. A few win; most don't. But the percentage is encouraging enough for the politician to take a chance, idle and utterly inconsequential as the life is.

Some of the Vice Presidents, such as Tom Marshall, fill the place with a philosophical detachment and amusement. Others, like Dawes, play a deeply-hidden but nevertheless potent rôle in legislative affairs. Both courses are impossible to Charley; the first, because he isn't detached or philosophical and has lost all sense of humor; and the second, because the political situation is against him.

He might be willing enough to dabble in the undercurrent, but the Hoover machine won't stand for any such meddling without a fight, and Charley never had a stomach for insurgency. The only time he covertly intruded he still remembers the chilly and tight-lipped hostility with which he was greeted about the White House when he came for the bi-weekly Cabinet conferences.

And as it was such a petty thing it required no imagination to picture what the Hooverian outrage would be should he really do something important.

Charley had merely loaned his official car to a group of Senate malcontents who called on Hoover to inquire how he stood on the Debenture Plan. To be asked to state his position, bluntly and unequivocally, was shock enough to the President. To learn that this outrage had been conveyed in Charley's official car was well nigh unforgivable.

Anyway, the indignation displayed by the President and his staff was enough to cure Charley. That little flyer in conspiracy was all he wanted of that sort of stuff.

But being a man who for many years had been in the midst of the political stew, Charley just had to do something—especially with those tireless complexes gnawing in him. If he couldn't be a philosopher, humorist, or conspirator, he could at least be a stern and unbending disciplinarian in the Senate and a defiant defender of Vice-Presidential rank and precedence there and elsewhere, particularly at social dinner tables.

It is easy to smile, and Charley's friends and former Senate colleagues have been gleefully doing that since he assumed his lofty rôle, but a heart-to-heart chat with him will prove that it is really no laughing matter.

He is profoundly and earnesly distressed at the condition in which he found the Vice Presidency, and until he goes up or out—the former preferably, of course—he intends devoting his time and strength advancing its fallen and sadly neglected estate.

If, by God's will, he must be content with the Vice Presidency, this labor of love and patriotism will be his self-sacrificing and lofty contribution to his native land. Laughter and raillery will daunt him not.

He proposes to force the Senate to decorum if he has to shatter gavels as fast as they can be made, and official society will bow to the majesty of his rank if he has to embarrass a thousand Secretaries of State.

"Might as well settle this thing once and for all," it is related he told a friend in a confidential moment. "You can never tell what will happen, and we might as well get this thing straightened out now."

It is what the psychologists call a defense mechanism, of course. But, as Charley might well say if he knew about such things, who is there without one? He is Vice President, and wants to be President. The odds are against him, for he is sixty-nine and Hoover is only fifty-five.

It is true that Hoover is fat, flaccid and worried and a dismal failure. But he has as yet never been seriously ill and Charley is not only fat but much older. Further, if the 1932 Republican nomination is worth anything, Hoover will get it. If it is not worth having, Charley doesn't want it.

So he has to content himself with day-dreaming about the Presidency—and meanwhile he tries to make the Vice Presidency as awe-inspiring and important as he knows how, even to the point of tossing aside the usual rules of courtesy between the two branches of Congress and encouraging the forthright and insurgent Norris, despite the shocked protest of that paragon of rigid immobility, Fess of Ohio, to speak bluntly and fittingly about the Republican crew of political mercenaries in the House.

To the social Old Guard of Washington, Charley and Dolly may be a riotous joke. But for the Vice President and his hefty and militant sister the others are a pack of snooty, strutting swells, who faze them not at all and with whom they are prepared to exchange blow for blow regardless of the shrieks of merriment from the onlookers and the outraged scowls of the stiff-backed Hoovers.

Principle is principle, and Alice Longworth and her crowd will take place after Charley and Dolly or, by God, they won't take place at all. In the Senate, Charley harries the chamber, demanding silence and order with a zeal and clamor that frightens the galleries and enrages the Senators, and in the evening, accompanied by the redoubtable Dolly, he raids and ravages dinner tables to satisfy their craving for precedence.

What matter if the world chortles in derision? By his vigor of conduct and the magnificence and array of his residences and office establishments shall they know him.

Charley's offices in the capital are to-day one of the most astounding sights of Washington. They are a cross between a giant tribal wickiup and a Sultan's seraglio. A section of one of the corridors of the Senate Office Building was blocked off to accommodate them. The corridor was converted into a lofty outer reception room and filled up with massive and glistening desks and chairs.

To the left are the chambers of his secretarial staff, of a number befitting so exalted a dignitary. These offices and ante-rooms are also equipped with new and lavish furnishings. To the right of the reception-room is Charley's official salon and the crowning glory of Capitol Hill.

It is impressively indicated by a chaste sign of three-inch gold lettering on a cherry background, reading "The Vice President." The room itself is the size of a manorial hall. A multitude of overstuffed chairs and lounges serve only to outline its vastness.

At the head of the cavern is a vast table of blockhouse dimensions, cherry red, as is all the rest of the furniture. What is probably one of the most curious throne chairs in the world faces it.

Its back is almost six feet in height, and is of carved and filigreed wood. At the top, in gilt letters, are the words, "The Chief." In the center is a plaque of carving. Around the rim of this piece of artistry is inscribed, also in gold lettering, the fact that the chair is the gift of the Original Curtis Boys and Matthew Quay Glaser.

Within are the mysterious words: KO-TNA-U-CA-SHE-THI-CE-XTSI-MO-KO-ONTHIA-ETTO-N, apparently some secret code, understood only by Charley and his brother tribesmen.

One wall is practically taken up by a ponderous book cabinet, the size of a corn-crib, with long panels of glass, all closely curtained. No sign of a book is visible.

Festooning the walls are numerous pen and ink cartoons of Charley, all complimentary, of course, the gifts of humble newspaper artists. A four-foot panorama of a great wheat field, a photograph of his log-cabin birthplace, so he claims, another of his former Topeka home and one of his present Topeka residence, and a picture of an Indian head are interspersed among the sketches. Indian moccasins, heavily beaded, and a miniature tepee are strewn about the huge marble mantelpiece.

In several corners stand banners. One, Charley explains, is the national standard that flew over the capitol the day he was inaugurated Vice President. The other is the Vice President's flag, the second ever made. The first, he relates, was made for Dawes and was taken away by him when he retired. Along one wall is a great over-stuffed leather couch, easily ten feet in length. Everything is as shiny as a mirror, twice as large as normal size, and as gaudy and ornate as a movie palace.

Charley takes a deep and stirring pride in the establishment. The interested caller is carefully shown all its wonders, and he modestly explains that it was all his own idea. Other Vice Presidents have had luxurious quarters, but it was he who conceived the idea of blocking up a whole corridor to make a throne room and of fitting it out with regal magnificence.

For years, as a member of Congress, Charley resided in an unostentatious dwelling in a modest residential section in Washington, but, elected to the Vice Presidency, he found it shabby and too meager.

Nothing less than the imperial suite of the fashionable Mayflower Hotel would do for him and the Ganns, meaning Dolly. There is a Mr. Gann, of course, but officially he is wholly inconsequential.

There is a good deal of mystery about this ten-room hotel apartment. For a while the story about town was that Charley got it rent free. When his social-precedence crusade was in its first bloom, reporters made inquiries of the management about the matter.

The hotel people were reluctant to discuss it, but persistent interrogation elicited certain details. It was learned that the regular rent of the apartment is $25,000 a year, but that since royalty comes to the capital only rarely, it had been used but infrequently.

From information obtained as to the number of days in the average year it had been occupied, the reporters calculated that it brought in about $7,500 annually. Taking Charley's and the manager's word that he really did pay rent, it was concluded that this figure was approximately what he got the suite for.

But the estimate is only a guess. Whatever the rental, the hotel apparently considers the difference between what it gets and what the place is listed for as fully compensated by the fact that the Vice President of the United States is one of its resident guests.

In fact, so satisfied is the management with the arrange-
ment, that it is understood to have offered Charley and Dolly
a private elevator. That is, when they entered one of the lifts
it would go up or down to their destination without stopping
for other calls. But Charley, ever the man of the people, declined this undue ostentation.

For him, only the simpler ways. He has no fear of brushing
elbows with his fellow-man.

When the reporters approached Charley about the question
of rent he went straight up in the air.

"It's nobody's —damned business what I pay," he roared at
them. "They made me a proposition and I accepted it. What
that is, is strictly between them and me."

Charley also strongly intimated that he knew the source of
all these malicious tales. And nothing would give him greater
pleasure, he added, than to break their necks.

The Vice Presidency, despite its endless social demands and
opportunities—and Dolly takes full advantage of them, thus
necessitating Charley's presence to safeguard her precedence—
has made a lonely man of him.

His days may be taken up with vigorous gavel wielding and
every night of the season filled with a dinner engagement, but
these are empty satisfactions to a man of his habits and in-
stincts. Even under ordinary circumstances to be relegated to
the Vice Presidency would be a hardship to a man who, for
a third of a century, was an active participant in the political
mêlée.

But his social crusading has withdrawn him still further
from the fellowship of his former senatorial colleagues. By
the very nature of this ruckus, he has been forced to assume a
certain standoffishness, and the cloak-room joking about this,
and even more about Dolly's pranks, of which he is fully
aware, has raised a wall between him and his one-time Senate
colleagues.

When the Senate ladies haughtily refused to make Dolly, as
she demanded, the president of their exclusive luncheon club,

friendly relations between Charley and a number of husband-Senators naturally did not flourish.

The Indian in him just can't help cropping out when a chance arises to hammer them out of order and curtly command them to take their places and keep quiet. The Senators in turn resent the rebuke, with the result that a below-the-surface but nevertheless most active feud rages between them and the Vice President.

As floor leader, Charley was constantly called upon by the reporters. Every day a score or more of them would seek him for information about plans, line-ups and dope. He liked to growl and grumble about their "starting things," but he enjoyed the contact thoroughly, and the pressmen considered him a pretty good scout.

But as Vice President the press gallery pays no attention to him, except to josh his social-gunning. The loss of his press relations distresses Charley deeply. He is bitter about old reporter friends who have written jokingly about his social activities, and if he should ever take up his residence in the White House many a newspaper home will languish in gloom waiting a bid to the sacred dinner-table.

Charley may not be a great engineer or humanitarian, he has not fed the children of Belgium nor did he put an end to an anarchistic uprising of Boston police, but in his way he, too, has an active sense of the spectacular. Witness his ten-room hotel suite in all its oriental-rug magnificence, to say nothing of silks and satins and numerous tinted-tiled bathrooms, and the regal opulence of his offices.

But it was during his campaigning that he really showed his stuff as an impresario of the dramatic. The travelling show he put on was one of the drollest staged in a Presidential race in a long time. The glamor of the big-top act that Al Smith produced caused Charley's carnival to be overlooked, but in its way it was a gem.

As a speaker, Charley was a total loss, but what he lacked in oratory or logic, he more than made up in showmanship. He didn't miss a trick, and, with the aid of the accommodating reporters acompanying him, he now and then got quite a play in the papers.

There was the time he pinched a few fingers in the door of an automobile and then bandaged his whole hand, hung it in a sling from around his neck and heroically announced that though stricken low nothing could keep him from his onslaught upon the foe. That play was worth quite a spread, with pictures.

Then there was the time he underwent a disconcerting heckling from a farmer who insisted on asking particularly obnoxious questions about Charley's and the Republican Party's record on fulfilling pledges to render aid and succor to agriculture. Angered by the effectiveness of the quizzing, Charley roared out that there was no use answering, as the interrogator was "too damned dumb to understand."

The Republican press made much of this incident, but no mention was ever made of the aftermath. The Smithites in the rural districts took to appearing at Charley's meetings with signs reading, "Farmers, you are too damned dumb to understand." Charley didn't like that at all.

When he first took to the stump he traveled in an ordinary Pullman car. But Sister Dolly waxed indignant at this, and one day hied herself over to "Doc" Work's office, where she bitterly berated the apologetic campaign director for the indignity that was being heaped upon Charley.

The campaign, she declared, was a Hoover-*Curtis* campaign, and don't you forget it. Hoover might be a great and good man, but so was Charley. He was just as good-looking as Hoover and they had better begin using his picture.

So Charley was given a private car, a press agent, a barker —introducer, was his official designation—and an Indian Princess.

Also his visage, with his scraggly mustache carefully and

neatly trimmed by this time, was plastered up by the side of Hoover's on all the official posters. Press associations were invited to send staff men on the car, and thus equipped, Charley finished out the campagin.

One of his missions was to line up the Indian vote. From Iroquois to Sioux and from Winnebago to Pueblo, they all took him into the fold, and presumably he won them all for the Republican ticket.

Charley had two neat acts for his appearances, depending on what kind of stop was made. At short back-platform turn-outs the barker and the Indian Princess did their stuff.

The spieler would appear at the rear of the car and in vigorous tones bark up the crowd. He would then present the Princess, who would warble a sad Indian melody that made ado over "Hi-o-hi-o-hi-o." The lady finished, Charley's broad smile would put in an appearance.

Sometimes there would be a few words from him, but whether he spoke or not there was always much handshaking. As the train pulled out, the Princess would wave farewell with a pretty flag. It was all simple, sweet and unaffected.

At the big evening meetings, held indoors, Charley had an-other effective gag. After the introductions, he stepped forward to speak; the band in the hall—primed in advance for the stunt—would break into "The Star-Spangled Banner."

Charley would instantly stiffen to attention and, of course, the mob would have to get out of its seats. When the music ceased, Charley would then pull a line that never failed to get a big hand.

"I want to thank the musicians," he would say, "for playing our glorious national anthem. I would far rather start my speeches to the strains of 'The Star-Spangled Banner' than to those of 'The Sidewalks of New York.'"

The campaign was the cause of Charley's being invested by reporters with the curious title of Egg Charley.

Since then some of the Washington correspondents have

debased the designation to other purposes, and it has now come to mean among them a certain state of alcoholic exuberation. Charley, it should be stated in all fairness, is in no way associated with this later development.

In the beginning, applied to him, the nickname arose out of a sort of satirical affection for him among the reporters who covered his Vice-Presidential medicine show. Being a staunch and unswerving Republican, he is naturally a high-tariff zealot. In all his speeches, he made much of the great benefits that have come to one and all from this great boon to mankind.

Getting down to particulars, he would relate in detail the important part he played from time to time in making possible its manifold blessings. There was the instance, he would tell, when the farmers came to him and begged him piteously to protect them from the ruinous inroads of oriental dried and frozen eggs. He was, it appeared, deeply moved by their pleas and indignation flamed in his breast against this subtle yellow peril.

He rose heroically to the occasion and through his indefatigable efforts a high impost was plastered upon the perfidious foreign products. But if Charley thought the fight was over he was mistaken.

After a time sinister interests approached him and with devious wiles attempted to play upon him to have the duty removed. The farmers, they said, no longer needed the protection.

But Charley was not to be taken in.

"You have come to the wrong Sen-a-toah," he would relate he had roared at them.

And they, taken aback, slunk back into the dark realms from which they had come. American eggs had been saved, and Charley rested modestly content with the great victory.

Always he would begin the recital of this saga with a fierce shout: "And what about eggs ... ?"

The effect of the outcry was always encouraging.

The by-this-time drowsing audience would be startled out of its dozing and with a fresh start Charley would tear into the gory details of his egg battle.

The reporters, amused at the antic, evolved the Egg Charley appellation, and it promptly spread far and wide, particularly in political circles. Naturally, it soon reached Charley's outraged ears.

After thinking it over he finally decided to drop the egg story. But every now and then he would forget, and casting about for something with which to bestir his drooping listeners, he would inadvertently yell at the point in his speech where formerly he would begin his egg tale:

"And what about ... ?"

He always caught himself in time and would veer off to something else.

Before he went on the stump, Charley had made few speeches in his life. In his twenty-odd years in the Senate he had not made over a half-dozen, if that many. In his campaigning in Kansas, his electioneering was almost entirely glad-hand and personal-contact work.

On his feet he is awkward and unhappy. When he took to the hustings he fixed up a speech and kept closely to it. He was one of the dullest of the campaign orators.

But what he lacked in eloquence he more than made up in sudden outbursts. It was as if he would get peeved with himself and bored with the crowd and take it out in an outbreak of roaring.

His address had a large number of references to the "flag we all love and revere" and there was much about home, mother, womanhood and that sort of thing. The publicity agents of the National Republican Committee got up press re leases that gave so-called extracts from his daily speeches.

These briefs ranged the entire scope of the campaign issues —that is, the ones that were talked about by the Republican candidates. Charley would make sufficient reference to the released press-matter to protect the reporters and then carry on with his regular harangue.

\*

THERE was a bit of Jacksonian touch to his beginnings, but he didn't live up to the promise of his early youth. He was a regular from the start. On his mother's side his ancestry goes back to White Plume, Chief of the Kaw tribe of Kansas Indians, to Pawhuska, a famous fighting Chief of the Osage tribe, and to a French trader, one Louis Pappan.

His father was the adventurous scion of a New England family who rose to a Captaincy in the Civil War. His mother died when he was three years old, and he was taken by his Grandmother Pappan, who lived on an Indian reservation, sixty miles west of Topeka.

There is a legend that while he was a boy on the reservation, the peaceful tribe heard that the Cheyennes had gone on the warpath, and that Charley was sent to summon aid. It is his sole martial adventure.

Later, he became a jockey and his love for horses remains one of his happiest traits. All his life he has been a frequenter of race-tracks, and be it said for him that this is one habit he has not changed since becoming Vice President.

Charley's fondness for the race-track was responsible for a really unfair accusation against him during the 1928 campaign. Senator Bruce of Maryland, an ardent wet, openly charged that he knew of an instance when Charley had pulled a flask from his hip and invited some friends with him to partake.

Bruce named names, and the fight was on. Charley vehemently denounced the accusation as a canard. The men mentioned were interviewed and they too denied the story. Charley really is not a drinking man. After his illness several years ago he was advised by his doctors to take a small drink daily as a tonic, and he did so, but only as a medicine. He does not care for liquor and he has never toted a flask.

In his personal life he has been as regular as in his political affairs. His one vice is a fondness for watching the thoroughbreds run. He never bets.

Charley got into politics soon after putting out his shingle as a lawyer. Topeka, though dry, had a hundred flourishing and wide-open saloons. The good folk grumbled loudly thereat and threatened a reform ticket.

The local bosses and saloon-keepers, casting about for a safe candidate who would at the same time mollify the respectable element, hit upon the youthful and ambitious Charley. They knew him for a good fellow, quiet and modest but no fanatic, and they felt they could safely entrust things in his hands.

So, backed by the wets and the drys, Charley was elected. He promised to enforce the law, which didn't disturb the politicians and satisfied the drys.

In office, with his eye on the congressional seat, and considerably, it is related, to the politicians' disgust, he proceeded to make good his pledges. He closed the saloons and went to Congress—again enthusiastically supported by both sides, the drys to reward him and the wets to get him out of the county.

He served in Congress, with the exception of a two-year period when the Populists defeated him, continuously from 1893 until his election to the Vice Presidency in 1928. He came to the Senate in 1907.

As Republican leader, following the death of Henry Cabot Lodge, Charley came to be known as the greatest whisperer in the history of Congress. Whenever he took his favorite pose, with a short fat arm coiled around another Senator's shoulders, the Press Gallery got busy. It was a sure sign that something was doing.

As floor leader he adhered to his dislike for speeches. "Talk, talk, talk," he would complain to the reporters about the endless Senate deliberations. He was one of the originators and most persistent sponsors of the cloture rule permitting a limit on Senate debate by means of a two-thirds vote.

It is his firm belief, borne out by extensive experience, that everything can be fixed by friendly and confidential getting together. As, of course, it usually is—despite the seas of words.

As a fixer Charley was one of the best in the business. He isn't much to look at—a little, fat, saffron-skinned man, with a round seal-like visage—and there is no affectation of culture or learning about him, but he was worth a dozen austere and disdainful Lodges in fixing things up.

Charley, as floor leader, had no illusions about his colleagues, but as long as he was one of them he didn't high-hat them. He got along agreeably with Republicans, Democrats and Insurgents.

Norris once said of him that "Charley Curtis' word is as good as gold."

From the very start of his congressional career he was a resourceful fixer. Czar Reed was boss and Speaker of the House when Charley was a beginner there. One day Charley dropped into Reed's office to see about some patronage matter and found a caucus of the leaders in progress.

He started to leave, but Reed called to him, "Indian, what do you know about this?" The gang was trying to frame a gold-standard bill and couldn't get together on a scheme.

Charley didn't know anything about the gold standard but he was fast on figuring out ways to fix things up. He suggested that the job be taken out of the hands of the crowd and turned over to a select and trusted committee.

The suggestion took well and was promptly acted upon, and thereafter Charley was recognized as a young man of promise.

Of course, he voted for the War, and like all the other regulars, said nothing about the Harding Administration's scandals. He followed Lodge in fighting the League of Nations, and Coolidge a few years later in voting adherence to the World Court—with reservations.

He didn't have any strong convictions either way about either question. Whatever the Party did he was for. As a matter of fact, he has never had any deep convictions about any issue. He isn't built that way.

He believes unquestioningly in the Republican Party, a high tariff, the flag, home, mother and the irresistible efficacy of small favors to constituents. Since his elevation to the Vice Presidency he has added slightly to this store of beliefs by becoming convinced of the social eminence of the office.

Charley knows more people in Kansas by their first names than any one else in the State, which is why he stayed in Congress for thirty-three years. William Allen White, likewise round and soft of belly and jowl, and like Charley a kindly man, once said of him, "For thirty-five years Charley Curtis had been depositing favors in the political bank and today he is drawing checks on them."

All his life, indeed, Charley has devoted himself to doing favors for good Kansas Republicans. His appeal has always been personal. In that capacity he is an affable, efficient, useful man, and as long as Kansas was his field and Congress his goal he could handle the situation.

But once smitten by ambition and racked by suppressed desires Charley lost his equilibrium. With the robes of purple dangling teasingly before him, he has trimmed his straggling hairs and scraggly lip-furze, keeps a pretty regular crease in his pants, and knots his neckties with care. He has taken up a permanent relation with a stiff topper. His good-natured and friendly growls have given way to an affected pronunciation and if he whispers it is only in his sleep.

Of late, a new cause for alarm has stricken him. A strong suspicion has arisen in his mind that if Hoover is renominated, he may not be his running mate.

The Hoover faction have made no secret of their disapproval of Dolly's social ambitions and Charley's outcries about precedence. Charley was only a makeshift in 1928 and, with time to prepare for the 1932 convention, they might well shelve him, if they can safely do so.

Charley is too clever a politician not to know what is going on in the Hoover camp. Neither he nor the President has any affection for each other. The whole matter rests on whether it profits Hoover more to keep or to drop Charley. Should he decide on some one else, Charley would have to go.

The realization of this situation adds no happiness to Charley's days. He can hope only that Hoover finds himself so beleaguered that he can't take any chances and will have to hold on to him.

But Charley is taking no chances. In this racking dilemma he is preparing for the worst by refreshing his wide Kansas contacts. Should he lose out on the Vice Presidency, Charley is determined not to languish but to seek his old Senate seat. A Democrat holds that now, but Charley is not discouraged. The seeds, the handshakes, the scores of favors of the past he is sure will not be forgotten.

In the meantime, he is carrying on unabated his labor of love of trying to make the Vice Presidency a potent and re- spected estate.

"Good-night," said Mrs. Ruth Hanna McCormick, and an old friend of Charley's, one evening in response to his thanks for a pleasant visit at her home. "Come again, Charley."

"Say," was the outraged rejoinder, "where do you get that Charley stuff? Don't you know I am Vice President now?"

# CHAPTER FIVE

## WRONG-HORSE HARRY

*A*FTER Herbert Hoover had spent two months of rather cramped and sometimes seasick life aboard a battleship for the purpose of wooing Latin America, he came back to the United States and appointed, as the member of his Cabinet responsible for continuing this courtship, the one man whose name more than any other was anathema to all Latin America.

It was not that Latin Americans knew anything at all about Henry Lewis Stimson. They did not know whether he was liberal or conservative, whether he had brains or was the world's worst dumb-bell, whether he parted his hair in the middle or was bald-headed. They only knew that he had represented President Coolidge in Nicaragua, and Nicaragua to them was the symbol of all that was ill-smelling about North American relations with Latin America. It did not make any difference what Henry L. Stimson had done in Nicaragua; it only mattered that he was there.

The day the news leaked out that Henry L. Stimson had been appointed Secretary of State, the press associations which feed the great newspapers of Buenos Aires, Santiago and Rio de Janeiro with some three thousand words of North-American news daily, devoted exactly that number of words to direct quotes from Henry L. Stimson's book on Nicaragua. The book was written as propaganda for the State Department in order to whitewash its maladroitness in that country, and was intended only for consumption in the United States. It did not go down well below the Rio Grande.

Probably there are few Secretaries of State who have got off to a less propitious start than Henry L. Stimson. In the first place, he was late arriving in Washington. After winding up his work as Governor General of the Philippines and after a slow trip across the Pacific, he found the Hoover Administration already four weeks in office with the State Department machinery, which Frank B. Kellogg, after two years of travail, had whipped into comparatively efficient shape, going at top speed. A revolution was ramping up and down Mexico. Europe was in the throes of formulating the Young Plan. Elihu Root had been in Europe drawing up a protocol by which the United States might slip quietly into the World Court; the League was preparing to convene its Preparatory Commission on Disarmament and the Coast Guard had just sunk the Canadian rum-runner, *I'm Alone,* two hundred and fifteen miles off the Louisiana Coast, in a manner which promised to make prohibition history.

Into all this, Henry L. Stimson, accustomed to working five-hour days, a multitude of servants and the leisurely ways of the tropics, was suddenly plunked. The result had to be either complete stoppage of the fast-whirling machinery of foreign affairs, or else the spectacle of Henry L. Stimson bumping along over the cogs trying to keep pace with the wheels.

What happened was a combination of both. The revolution in Mexico, the formulation of the Young Plan and the indignation of the Canadian people at the sinking of the *I'm Alone* could not be slowed up despite Mr. Stimson's inexperience, and so, in these cases, Mr. Stimson went bumping along on the cogs of the machinery of foreign affairs, trying to keep up with the outside world. Regarding matters of lesser importance or those over which the United States had some power of initiation or control, Mr. Stimson pretty effectively applied the brakes.

One of the first obsessions he acquired after arriving in Washington was that certain people, more particularly the press and the bureau of press relations, were lying awake nights planning to knife him when his back was turned. As a result he issued an order that no news could be released to the press without his approval. And such fear did the new Secretary of State inspire in his subordinates that in one case such routine handouts as a birthday message to the President of Uruguay and an announcement of American participation in a Pan-American Infant Hygiene Conference were held up two days awaiting Mr. Stimson's return from a week-end.

Week-ends of the British variety, which begin early Friday and do not end until Tuesday morning, were Mr. Stimson's regular diversion during his first summer in Washington, and they contrasted rather disastrously with Frank B. Kellogg's habit of fretting and fuming at his desk literally day and night without vacation for four years.

Despite this, it was Mr. Stimson's constant but good-natured complaint that Mr. Hoover was working him too hard. Mrs. Stimson was not so good-natured about it. She told her friends that Mr. Hoover was a slave driver. Comparatively speaking, he was. The gentleman who sat in the White House across the street had become accustomed, as a big corporation head, to prodigious effort and he expected it of others. Mr. Stimson's long week-ends got no Presidential sympathy.

Nor did they get much sympathy from any one else. On one particular Saturday morning when important news regarding revision of German War payments to the United States had been received at the State Department, Mr. Stimson informed the press that he could not meet with them at the scheduled hour because he was engaged in "work for the President." Half an hour later, he appeared on the White House tennis court clad in immaculate flannels. The President was not there.

Next morning the newspapers published a detailed account of the importance which Mr. Stimson attached to his membership in the "Tennis Cabinet"; how he had hired, at State Department expense, an extra Negro messenger whose job it was to bring his tennis clothes down to the Department in the afternoon and lay them out in the dressing room adjoining his office, and how the Secretary, after donning them, put himself at the head of the "Tennis Parade"—Regnier his aide, Keatley, his personal stenographer, and Roach, his valet,—while guards saluted and salaamed.

For two years Mr. Stimson never missed another press conference without valid excuse.

Finding that things were happening all around him, about which he knew nothing, Secretary Stimson issued an order that each political division of the State Department should report to him daily on the work it had accomplished. Nonpolitical divisions, such as the Passport Bureau, the Visa Office, the Personnel Office, that of the Solicitor, he required to report twice a week. The result was that on Wednesdays and Saturdays almost every one in the State Department was so busy writing reports to the Secretary that nothing much else was accomplished. The stenographic division was swamped, and Mr. Stimson himself carried home with him a stack of reports which every one surmised were thrown in the waste basket like so many uncorrected examination papers.

All of which did not add materially to the efficiency of the State Department and created the general impression among his subordinates that Henry L. Stimson was a high-handed executive with military ideas and a propensity for giving orders which he had inherited from his days as Secretary of War.

This, of course, was a "spot" impression, created at that very unfair period when Mr. Stimson was green and when the State Department was dealing with some of the most important matters before it in years.

\*

Two years have passed since that hectic period. The State Department functions much more serenely now. Its personnel have more confidence in their chief and chafe less at his whims and eccentricities. But even to-day, Henry Lewis Stimson remains an enigma to most of those around him. He favors universal military conscription, yet was the most hard-hitting enemy the militarists had when they opposed a naval reduction treaty. He paid $800,000 for a palatial estate in fashionable Northwest Washington, yet he believes in the redistribution of wealth and advocates increased income taxes for the wealthy. He is cold, aloof, criticized as being snobbish, but does the most generous and thoughtful things for those around him. He is a strange mixture of conservatism and liberalism, of pacificism and militarism, of gentility and democracy.

The secret of this contradiction is Stimson's family. He has never been able to forget the proud part it played in the founding of these United States. He tries to forget; he tries to mix with his fellow-men; but never has he been able completely to divorce himself from the inherent instinct that he is of a race born to rule.

This instinct was first planted when John Stimson, fifth great-grandfather of Henry Lewis Stimson, born in England in 1605, came to America in the *Truelove,* settling at Watertown Farms. His son, George Stimson, having moved to Ipswich, Massachusetts, took down his rifle and powder horn to fight the Indians in King Philip's War. The latter's grandson, also named George, served as a Captain in the French and Indian and in the Revolutionary Wars, later returning to Windham, New York, in which State the Stimsons ever since have dabbled in politics, made money and been proud to live.

The first Henry Stimson, great-grandfather of Henry Lewis, born 1772, was one of the few Stimsons who has not been a fighting man. However, Stimson's father, Lewis Atterbury, made up for it by serving as a Captain and aide-de-camp in the Civil War.

By this time the family had accumulated a considerable fortune. Henry Clark Stimson, grandfather of Henry Lewis, born 1813, had become a wealthy banker and railroad president just at the period when the Morgans, the Harrimans and the Hills were making railroad history in the United States. Stimson's father, therefore, was under no compulsion to earn a living. He studied medicine, became Professor of Surgery at the Cornell Medical School and eventually built up a lucrative practice among New York's Four Hundred. He was known as New York's most fashionable physician and was as popular for his yacht racing as he was for his prescriptions. Few were the summers when he did not enter his yacht in the Trans-Atlantic race. For a while he held the record for this contest.

Young Henry Lewis Stimson was born into a stultifying world of wealth and luxury. He had no particular reason for worrying about the problem of making a living, and his early youth was not calculated to inspire such worry. While an undergraduate at Yale, he spent his vacations in what is an expensive luxury even for the sons of Eli—big-game hunting. He made annual excursions to the Rockies or to Canada and later gained some reputation for himself as the first white man to climb "The Chief" in the Glacier National Park. He interspersed these hunting trips with vacations in New Brunswick, Quebec and Switzerland, where he climbed the Matterhorn and the Rothhorn. Graduated from Yale in 1888, Stimson was, with two exceptions, like any other rich man's son who has a pipe-line to his father's purse and a desire to satisfy his curiosity.

These two exceptions were: family pride and an uncle.

Family pride has been the outstanding characteristic of all Stimsons since John Stimson crossed from England in the *Truelove*. Next to the pride they have taken in their family they have been proud of their country and their State. The State of New York they have considered a community corporation in which every Stimson must play his part. The United States they have considered only slightly less so. Therefore, it was incumbent upon young Henry Lewis to uphold the tradition of the Stimsons by upholding its pride in the Nation and the State.

Henry Albert Stimson, now ninety years old, and uncle of Henry Lewis, had felt this way. But instead of giving his life to the healing of the sick and the racing of yachts, as did Henry Lewis's father, he had dedicated it to the work of the Lord. He raised seven children, preached from pulpits in Minneapolis, St. Louis and New York, and became the outstanding and most liberal Congregationalist divine of his day.

In the life of Henry Lewis Stimson, his namesake, the Reverend Doctor Stimson played a great part—probably the most important part any individual has played. Young Henry Lewis took his problems to his uncle. They saw much of each other. Even to-day, when the present Secretary of State makes hurried business trips to New York, he seldom fails to spend an evening with the aged divine, and his uncle in turn never hesitates to sign his name to lengthy petitions urging the Secretary of State to take certain steps in international relations which other members of the State Department consider rank heresy.

From his uncle, therefore, Henry Lewis Stimson got a certain humanitarian and idealistic slant on life which, together with his family pride and his luxurious youth, made his character, even in its formative period, a combination of weird contradictions.

Dominant in his character was the inbred belief that being a Stimson, blessed with the privileges of wealth and prestige, he was born to rule. This rule, however, thanks to the teachings of a kindly uncle, was to be beneficent and for the good of the people. Mixed up with this were all the characteristics which ordinarily accrue from a life of luxury. Stimson was mentally and physically lazy. He had never been compelled to work. He was surrounded by conservative friends and conservative influences. Yet despite this environment, and partly because of his uncle, young Henry Lewis was able to keep a liberal and detached view on life such as most wealthy young men lost before they were graduated from knee breeches.

With this groundwork of character, Henry Lewis Stimson started out on a life that was to make him more renowned and more criticized than any of his distinguished ancestors.

*

WHEN Stimson, Governor General of the Philippines, was summoned to Washington to become Secretary of State, a friend wrote of him in the New York *Times*:

" 'The stern Daughter of the Voice of God' has stood ever at his elbow, laying on him the compulsions that she laid on men of old. * * * You saw him bow his head when the call came and sail away like a Roman proconsul. * * * It is as if some one out of the Good Book had put his hand on Stimson's shoulder with the familiar words, 'Well done, good and faithful servant.' "

Those words convey most accurately the impression which Mr. Stimson gives to the casual observer. On his face is the look of bored martyrdom. He, a Stimson, has been summoned to accept the responsibilities of his patriotism and his position, and he is not one to spurn the challenge....

The facts, however, belie both the look on Stimson's face and his friend's description quoted above.

Mr. Stimson became Secretary of State not at the command of the "Stern Daughter of the Voice of God," nor at the urging of some one out of the Good Book, but because his law partner, Elihu Root, and his old friend, William Howard Taft, were back in Washington pulling the wires for his appointment.

In fact, it has been the "Stern Daughter of the Voice of God" in the person of Elihu Root that has got for Mr. Stimson many of those important positions which, to the initiated, appear to be the reward of great merit plus the discernment of God. It was Elihu Root, a former Secretary of War, who recommended young Mr. Stimson for that post in 1911. It was Elihu Root who suggested him to Theodore Roosevelt as District Attorney for Southern New York in 1906, and, probably most important of all, it was Elihu Root who gave young Stimson his first job.

Also from an old and distinguished New York family, Root believes that old and distinguished New York families should stick together, and when Henry Lewis was 26 years old, a graduate of Yale and of Harvard Law School, Root took him into his law firm. Root's solicitude permitted young Stimson to marry Mabel Wellington White, who can trace her ancestry back even further than Stimson's to the first voyage of the *Mayflower*. Stimson did not particularly need to work to support a wife, but it was considered the more respectable thing to do. As soon as Stimson entered Root's firm, therefore, the marriage took place.

The cases which came across Stimson's desk as a member of the firm of Root and Clarke were the usual routine work of championing big business upon which most New York law firms fatten, and there was no indication during this period that young Mr. Stimson was any less conservative or more idealistic than the average scion of wealth and aristocracy.

After twelve years of private law practice, however, Theodore Roosevelt, himself a scion of wealth and aristocracy, believing as Root did, that such scions should stick together, appointed Stimson, still in his thirties, District Attorney for Southern New York. For the first time, Stimson showed flashes of the liberal background his uncle had helped instill in him. It was in the heyday of Roosevelt's trust-busting boom and Stimson, inspired by all the righteous wrath of his Puritan soul, went for the Sugar Trust. Having made a name for himself on this, he prosecuted Charles W. Morse, accused of misappropriating funds from the National Bank of America.

For a politician, it was a heaven-sent opportunity. Whether Stimson realized this or not, his prosecution of Morse won for him the Republican nomination for the governorship of his State.

There is some difference of opinion as to whether picking Stimson for this fight was a real act of friendship on Roosevelt's part. John A. Dix, experienced Democrat, was running as the Tammany candidate and was sure of election. However, some one had to run against him, and Stimson was picked as the goat. Only forty-three years old and a comparative babe as far as politics were concerned, he never had a chance. However, family pride, the inherent feeling that a Stimson is born to serve his country and rule it well, urged him on.

The result would have been laughable had it not been so tragic. Here was a wealthy young aristocrat never having felt the pinch of hunger, never having soiled his hands with manual labor, never having mingled with his fellow-men, pitted against a rough-and-tumble political fighter in an election whose success depended upon winning the toughest elements of Brooklyn and East-Side New York. His cultured accent, his uneasy platform presence, his cold personality, almost every detail of his manner betrayed his birth and breeding, gave his electorate an impression of a young aristocrat who condescends to rule, and who, though he may be a good ruler, condescends.

The opposition press called him the "human icicle." Then, after a half-dozen speeches, during which Stimson never varied his theme of "I stand squarely behind the policies of Theodore Roosevelt," and after Roosevelt had referred to him endearingly as "his" candidate, the nickname was changed to "Our Harry."

Stimson's failure as a glad-hander, brought to light so glaringly during the New York gubernatorial campaign, has remained a real handicap throughout his life. He is naturally cold and aloof, but not nearly so much so as he appears. At times he tries desperately to overcome this handicap. As Secretary of State he is constantly inviting people out to his colonial residence to chat and get acquainted. On these occasions he tries with almost visible effort to pull himself out of his shell, to radiate charm and personality. But he is a slow and diffident conversationalist, would rather sit in front of a fire with Mrs. Stimson and a book, and, on the whole, he fails. In Washington, the Diplomatic Corps, the State Department personnel, his Cabinet friends, all respect him and like him in a mild sort of way, but there is no enthusiasm. The inescapable fact is that Henry L. Stimson was born an aristocrat, and despite a kindly democratic soul, he never has been nor ever will be able to escape from perpetually giving the appearance of an aristocrat.

Although Stimson's personality plus his political ineptitude caused a Democratic landslide for John A. Dix, his efforts were not unrewarded. Theodore Roosevelt never forgot his friends, and a few months after his political defeat, Roosevelt and Root persuaded Taft to appoint Stimson Secretary of War. He was one of the youngest men ever to fill that office.

Although Stimson served for only two years as Secretary of War, he probably enjoyed it more than any other office he has held. The army at that time had not reached the impressive peace-time proportions that it has since the "war to end war," and the Department to a considerable extent ran itself. Something which he may have inherited from the ancestors who fought in the early wars of the nation has always endeared the pomp and ceremony of military life to Henry L. Stimson, and in the War Department he felt very much at home. Also, he liked the high-ranking Generals who surrounded him. He considered them extremely capable and let them run his Department pretty much as they pleased.

Mr. Stimson, therefore, had time to enjoy some of the luxuries he had indulged in during his early youth. He rode in Rock Creek Park every morning, frequently wearing his riding boots to his office after the custom of young aristocrats in those days. It was at that time that he won the nickname, "Light-Horse Harry," and one of the most striking pictures which graces the ante-room of the Secretary of War to-day is a full-length portrait of Henry Lewis Stimson, breeches, boots, crop and all.

After the disruption of the Taft-Roosevelt honeymoon had thrown Mr. Taft out of the White House in 1913, Mr. Stimson went back to New York, and with the exception of some help which he gave Al Smith in reforming the State Constitution in 1915, applied himself rather assiduously to his law practice and to building up a fortune. He acquired Highold, an expansive estate on Long Island. He went in for fox-hunting. He ruled over his little suburban world like any twelfth-century feudal lord.

After fifteen years of this, the fortune was built, the practice was thriving and Mr. Stimson had sunk rather successfully out of the public eye. So far had he sunk that when he came back with a reverberation which put his name on the cables to all parts of the world, every newspaperman handling the story had to scratch his head and run to *Who's Who* to find out just who Henry Lewis Stimson was.

The reverberation occurred in 1927, when the Coolidge Administration had got itself into more trouble in one small country than had any other administration in years, and needed a man to straighten out the mess. Colonel Stimson, as he was then called, was drafted as President Coolidge's personal representative in Nicaragua.

Just how he happened to be drafted, Mr. Stimson himself does not know. Most people suspect Root and Taft. Stimson was in the middle of an important law case, when the "Stern Daughter of the Voice of God" called up in the form of Frank B. Kellogg and asked him to come to Washington. Stimson protested. At that particular time he was getting a little tired of the martyr complex. Partly because it was a call from the President, however, partly because his curiosity was aroused, Stimson came.

Calvin Coolidge gave him laconic instructions to go to Nicaragua and straighten out the mess Kellogg had got into.

Stimson demurred. But he did not demur very vigorously. At heart he was flattered that the long list of services which the Stimsons had rendered their country was to be made longer. So he made only one condition with the President, namely, that he, Stimson, should have complete authority to do whatever he found necessary once he arrived in Nicaragua. Coolidge agreed.

Mr. Kellogg, however, was not so amenable. While Stimson was on the high seas, Mr. Kellogg began to fidget. He began to conjure up all kinds of mistakes which the Special Representative of the President might make when confronted with the pitfalls of Nicaraguan jungles and politics. Finally, fidgety Mr. Kellogg sent a telegram to head off Mr. Stimson at Managua. The telegram surrounded him with buts, ifs, whereases and warnings against the further use of American armed force in Nicaragua and against any pledge to guarantee Nicaraguan elections. Mr. Stimson, however, completely ignored this. He sent a telegram to the White House saying that he still assumed full authority to do whatever he considered expedient, and once again Calvin Coolidge replied in the affirmative.

Stimson took this literally. At one time he pledged, in effect, the entire military and naval force of the United States to make Jose M. Moncada, Nicaraguan rebel leader, lay down his arms. He did exactly what Mr. Kellogg did not want him to do. He promised that American marines would remain in Nicaragua and that they would guarantee a free and fair election.

Whether Mr. Stimson was wise in using this force and in making this pledge is for historians to decide. There is no question, however, that he substituted a definite policy for one of Kellogg vacillation and there is no question, also, that Calvin Coolidge was pleased. It was because Mr. Coolidge was pleased that he sent Mr. Stimson to the Philippines, where a somewhat similar mess needed to be straightened out.

*

No situation could have been better ordered to the kindly despotism of the Stimson family than that which existed in the Philippines at that time. For six years the Philippines had been handled with the mailed and military fist of General Leonard B. Wood. Wood had been abrupt and peremptory. He had vetoed the bills of the Philippine legislature on a wholesale scale and almost without explanation. He had surrounded himself with the famous "Cavalry Cabinet"—military men who had become so biased against any human being with a brown skin that their advice was impossible. They believed that the way to keep a native in his place was to apply the tip of the toe to the seat of his pants. They drew a strict color line even to the point of prohibiting football matches between Filipinos and white service teams, for fear white prestige would lose "face" by defeat. Filipino political leaders—even the President of the Senate and the Speaker of the House—were considered too lowly to attend Government House receptions. They had so many mistresses, it was explained, that it was socially impossible to decide upon the correct wife to invite.

Into this situation walked a man whose ancestral lineage was so secure that he could afford to mingle with people far below him and who believed it his duty to mingle, a man who had been reared with the idea that he was born to rule but that his rule must be kindly, considerate and fair.

Mr. Stimson started from the premise that the Philippine Islands existed chiefly for the benefit of the Filipino people, not for the benefit of American business, not for the purpose of giving the United States a naval base in Pacific waters, and not for the aggrandizement and glory of the American empire. Once the Filipino politicos appreciated that premise, they were with him one hundred per cent. Mr. Stimson initiated a régime of full and frank discussion. His aim was to secure what he wanted by persuasion and coöperation rather than by force. On the whole he was successful. But at heart always the aristocratic despot, he never relinquished his final whip hand. If, after discussion, argument and persuasion, he could not get what he wanted, the army and navy of the United States were always at his command.

His first act was to fire the Cavalry Cabinet. His second was to invite Filipinos and their wives to Government House. The American colony never forgave him, and any Governor who offends the American colony can be rated, *ipso facto,* as having independence, courage and the interests of the Philippine people fundamentally at heart.

So there grew up between Stimson and the Philippine leaders a genuine affection, which continued long after the Governor-General relinquished his palace at Malaccan and came to Washington. Even as Secretary of State he made special trips to Congress to fight the sugar tariff and once caused deep resentment in the Diplomatic Corps by entertaining a Filipino delegation before he condescended to invite any foreign diplomat to his table.

When he finally sailed away from Manila in the spring of 1929, there was no question that Henry Lewis Stimson left behind him one of the best jobs he had ever done.

*

AFTER Secretary Stimson had weathered a rather severe initiation during his first few months in the State Department, the weird mixture of liberalism and conservatism, of pacifism and militarism, which makes up his character, began to crop out.

His first important step was the appointment of the late Joseph P. Cotton as Under-Secretary of State. Cotton was a thorough liberal. Where Stimson's liberalness balked, when it got too far away from the home base of conservative birth and wealthy environment, Cotton never stopped at anything. He was a man who not only would have been glad to have defended Rosika Schwimmer in her citizenship fight before the Supreme Court, but publicly boasted of it. Furthermore, Cotton was gifted with rare executive ability, and Stimson, wise enough to realize this and himself inherently a little lazy, let him run the Department.

The two men worked in closest harmony. Whether Stimson or Cotton was responsible for turning over many of the old precedents, set up as sacred under the Kellogg-Hughes régimes, it is difficult to say; but at any rate, between Cotton's restless energy and Stimson's placid liberalness, they were knocked down one by one.

The first to go was the ban against the dread Count Karolyi, whom the nervous Frank B. Kellogg had barred from the United States as a red menace. The wisdom of the Stimson move was promptly demonstrated by the pathetic way in which the poor Count proved a complete flop except at the tea tables of earnest old ladies and other innocuous worshippers of foreign titles.

Later Stimson did not bat an eye when the patrons of patriotism threw up their hands in horror because he had given a passport to Dorothy Detzer, militant pacifist, despite the fact that she declined to take an oath swearing to defend the Constitution with traditional rifle and pitchfork.

When it became apparent that descendants of American Negroes who founded the Republic of Liberia as a haven of freedom were selling their black brothers at $15 a head for the plantations of King Alfonso, Stimson pushed an investigation of it, and later sent the President of the Black Republic the most scathing diplomatic rebuke which the United States has sent any nation since it declared war on Germany. Later through Cotton's foresight, he headed off another slave scandal in Abyssinia by getting advance guarantees from the J. G. White Corporation that no slave labor would be used in the construction of the Lake Tsana dam at the mouth of the Blue Nile.

One of the most surprising things about Stimson was the way he meticulously refrained from following his predecessors' practice of raining a steady stream of pokes and punches at Soviet Russia. He had ample provocation. Maxim Litvinoff's scathing chastisement of his attempt to prevent war in Manchuria gave Stimson ample excuse to hit back.

Furthermore, he did not join in the chorus when the Pope broadcast his castigation of Russia, nor did he approve the suggestion of the man he worships most, Elihu Root, that the United States create an agency to guard against Soviet propaganda. Finally it became apparent that Mr. Stimson had certain sympathies with Soviet Russia; that while he did not condone the communist system, he did believe that somewhere in between the extremes of Russian communism and American capitalism there might be a happier utopia; that while he did not approve Russia's forcible confiscation of property, he did believe that the tremendous concentration of wealth in the hands of a few was a decided handicap to the welfare of the United States and that a more equable distribution of wealth was absolutely necessary.

It was these ideas which led him to order a thorough research and study of everything Russian—a study to be made not by the career diplomats who for years had been manufacturing Bolshevist bogies for Frank B. Kellogg, but by outsiders who had not lost their vision and perspective.

Finally, Stimson has constantly kept a weather eye on the wealthy social clique which long has dominated the foreign service. Before he took office, his liberal friends warned him of the pitfalls these gentlemen could place in his path, and he has been suspicious of the Butler Wrights, the Joe Grews, the Hugh Wilsons and all the others ever since. Almost immediately he assumed office, he gave them one of the most subtle but position-putting pieces of punishment ever meted out to the career service.

It occurred at the first diplomatic tea held at Woodley. It is the usual custom at these functions for the wives of the various Assistant Secretaries to assist the wife of the Secretary of State in pouring. These ladies are Mrs. Wilbur Carr, Mrs. William R. Castle, Jr., and Mrs. Frances White—all charming, acquainted with the Diplomatic Corps, and socially secure. Mr.

Stimson, however, had heard that the career service was coming to view these functions as their own, so he reversed the process. He selected Mrs. Ruth B. Shipley, Miss Margaret M. Hanna, and one or two other equally efficient but none-too-social ladies who had worked their way up from clerkships to the rank of bureau chiefs, and he put them behind the tea-pots.

A lot of things happened that aren't supposed to happen at the usual well-oiled diplomatic tea. For one thing, Captain Regnier, Stimson's young and precocious military aide, did the announcing and got the Minister of Bolivia mixed up with the Minister of Sweden, which was no compliment to the latter. And when the Italian Ambassadress wanted her car she had to wait thirty minutes for it. But for the most part, the party delighted a great number of people who do not usually experience much delight at diplomatic receptions and it performed the wholesome function of putting the career corps decidedly in its place.

*

WHILE Henry Lewis Stimson was being labeled revolutionary and radical by the career corps in regard to Count Karolyi, Liberia and Russia, he was being bull-headed, militaristic and inept in handling a score of other things, including Brazil, Fascism and Major-General Smedley Butler.

Fundamentally, Mr. Stimson is as honest as he tries to be fair. He has two definite handicaps, however. One is an exceedingly bad memory. The other is a temper. On occasion, Mr. Stimson has completely lost control of the latter. He has sputtered, fumed and issued red-hot statements which focused public attention upon his difficulties. Very few people in the United States ever would have heard of the Washington *Post's* insult to Prince de Ligne, the Belgian Ambassador, had not Stimson publicly denounced it. Nor would any one have cared a tinker's dam whether he was properly consulting with the Secretary of the Navy during the Japanese naval negotiations, had not Stimson, grim-lipped and white-faced, bitterly denounced a Washington *Post* editorial saying that he was neglecting the navy.

Like his temper, Mr. Stimson's memory is constantly playing him tricks. Once he announced that he had sent a telegram instructing the American Ambassador in Havana to take up with the Cuban Government the long controverted claims of Joseph E. Barlow. After the newspapers had featured this on their front pages, Mr. Stimson had to announce next day that he had made a mistake, that no telegram had been sent to Havana, and that he had been thinking of a telegram he sent to Berlin in regard to the Orloff case, in which Russian forgers had linked Senator Borah with Soviet conspirators.

It was not a faulty memory, however, that has sometimes caused Mr. Stimson, his back to the wall, to issue what is referred to in polite circles as a diplomatic denial, but which among the more hard-fisted is known as an ordinary variety of cheap garden lie.

Every foreign office in Europe issues them—on the average of two or three times a week. But American diplomacy has so boasted of its own chastity and Mr. Stimson has been given such a character of aristocratic saintliness, that it surprised some of his friends to hear Rear-Admiral Hilary P. Jones inform a Senate committee under oath that he had told Mr. Stimson he would not go to London, whereas Mr. Stimson had previously told the press that Admiral Jones had told him no such thing. Again it jarred some of those not conversant with the wiles of diplomacy to hear Mr. Stimson say that the Canadian Minister, Vincent Massey, had never expressed alarm over American tariff increases, whereas Senators Borah and Watson said that Mr. Stimson had told them quite a contrary story.

It was neither faulty memory nor entirely a desire to deceive, however, which led Mr. Stimson into his imbroglio in regard to Brazil. It was just plain bull-headedness. The Solicitors of the State Department—having devoted entire lives to studying international law—had informed their Secretary of State that there was no provision under international law requiring him to declare an arms embargo against Brazilian revolutionaries. After receiving this advice, Mr. Stimson stepped into the next room and informed the press that he was placing an embargo on arms shipments to Brazil. He maintained that international law required this.

Unfortunately, Mr. Stimson was right but didn't know it. The United States and Brazil both had ratified a multi-lateral treaty some four months before making such an embargo obligatory, but Mr. Stimson didn't know it existed and the bright young men who advise him had forgotten about it.

Forty-eight hours after declaring this embargo, the Brazilian Government, which Mr. Stimson had sought to keep in power, was overthrown.

Thereafter, Stimson's old nickname was changed to "Wrong-Horse Harry."

He has been trying to explain his Brazilian mistake ever since. During the course of one of these explanations, before the Council of Foreign Relations, Mr. Stimson cited the arms treaty as justification for his embargo, but failed to mention the rather relevant point that he did not know of its existence at the time.

It was also bull-headedness that got Secretary Stimson into such a mess with those two poles of personality, Benito Mussolini and Smedley Butler. Stimson had supported Hoover in his demand that the stormy petrel of the Marine Corps be court-martialed instead of merely reprimanded as punishment for calling the Premier of Italy a hit-and-run driver.

After the court martial had been ordered and there had been ample time to gauge the nation-wide abuse which it was heaping on the Hoover Administration, an emissary of General Butler's approached Stimson suggesting the court martial be abandoned. He found the Secretary of State in a mood reminiscent of the days when he was Secretary of War—of the days when his great-grandfathers had taken down their rifles to fight in King Philip's War, the French and Indian War, the Revolutionary War and the Civil War. Mr. Stimson pounded on the table. He puffed out his chest. He swore that General Butler was a soldier and would have to take a soldier's medicine.

He did not then know how much he was to regret that moment of militarist indignation!

A day or two later the Italian Ambassador himself came to ask that the court martial be abandoned and it was Stimson's turn to send an emissary to General Butler. He found the General's attorney, Major Henry Leonard, the coolest poker player he had ever encountered.

Stimson made his first move—a proposal that instead of a court martial, Butler be reprimanded, removed from his command and placed on the list awaiting orders. Leonard laughed in the emissary's face.

Stimson made his second move—a proposal that Butler be reprimanded, removed from his command and sent to Guam instead of being put on the list awaiting orders. Leonard laughed again.

Stimson made his third move—a proposal that Butler be reprimanded, continue his command, but write a letter of apology to the Italian Government. Leonard refused. Then he played his trump card. He sent word to Stimson that enough time had been wasted, that Butler had witnesses whom he had to subpoena from Italy, and that he would give Stimson only twelve hours more in which to offer a suitable compromise.

Stimson then made his last move. He asked what terms Butler wanted. The reply was: "Butler gets off with a mild reprimand, and he writes it himself."

The terms were accepted.

This was the second time Mr. Stimson had gone wrong where Mussolini was concerned. At the height of his clean-up of Kellogg's moth-eaten imperialistic policies, Mr. Stimson's attention was called to the fact that Mussolini's Ambassador in the United States, together with his consuls, had been promoting a reign of terror among Italo-Americans. Mussolini's envoys had been endeavoring to collect taxes from them. They had tried to prevent their naturalization as American citizens. They had spread Fascist propaganda among American schools, in one case causing the dismissal of a school teacher who refused to use the propaganda supplied her. And they had insisted that all Italians join and contribute to the Fascist League of North America.

Stimson ordered an investigation. But it was carried out under the direction of William R. Castle, Jr., then Assistant Secretary, whose best friend is Ambassador Martino and who gives to Fascism the same respectful reverence that his missionary ancestors divided between the Bible and the acquisition of land from Hawaiian natives.

The result was a white-wash of both Mussolini and his representatives in the United States. Mr. Stimson could not help knowing that Castle's investigation was violently partisan. But as a result of his birth and background, Mr. Stimson has a certain respect for established order, especially when it is in the form of a high-powered and successful dictatorship with which he is trying to negotiate a naval agreement. So he saved for Liberia and Nicaragua the invective which Mussolini justly had coming to him, and accepted the Castle report.

*

THERE is nothing more confusing about Henry Lewis Stimson than the fact that despite his naïve and tenacious worship of the folderol of militarism, he is a devout disciple of peace. A constant struggle goes on within him between reverence for the military exploits of his ancestors and the pacifist ideals implanted by his benign uncle. The former found expression in his youth when he became an enthusiastic member of the crack cavalry regiment of the New York National Guard. It found expression again when war was declared. Stimson had attended Plattsburg, got a commission as a First Lieutenant and was one of the first to enlist. But to have a former Secretary of War rank no higher than a Lieutenant was most embarrassing, and Pershing very soon assigned him to the 305th Field Artillery with the rank of Colonel. Like all Stimsons, he served faithfully, though not brilliantly, saw real service in France and won the respect and devotion of his men.

After the War was over, after he had become Secretary of State, even after he had participated in ceremonies commemorating a Pact Renouncing War, Stimson showed how deeply implanted is his devotion to the military by declaring his views on compulsory military training unchanged—that now, as before the War, every young man in the United States should be compelled to spend several precious months carrying a rifle around a dusty parade-ground for the honor, glory and defense of his country.

Despite all this, Mr. Stimson considers himself a devout disciple of peace. He makes this declaration so often that he gives the impression he is chiefly trying to convince himself of his own pacifism. And while Henry Lewis Stimson would become an outright pacifist only if he, himself, could perpetually dictate the terms of peace, he does have very genuine but poorly managed impulses in that direction.

The two outstanding examples are his effort to uphold the Kellogg Treaty in Manchuria and the London Naval Conference.

Stimson's attack on naval disarmament had been painstakingly planned. He stumbled into the Manchurian row by accident. Although it is not generally appreciated, Stimson probably did a better job in Manchuria than at London.

In dealing with the crisis in Manchuria, Stimson showed more nerve than he has displayed in tackling any other problem. Although the slap which he got from Litvinoff for his pains resounded with such a whack that it drowned the real effect of his work, actually Stimson ended a near war in the Far East and a slap in the face is not an exorbitant price to pay for that.

Possibly if Mr. Stimson had known the Senate in those earlier days as he does now, he would have been more cautious. The principle of what he did went diametrically against the grain of what a majority of the Senate has stood for during a century of isolation. Manchuria was some 6,000 miles away. Only about $12,000,000 worth of American property and a score of Jewish-American fur-buyers are located in the entire area and they were nowhere near the scene of the dispute.

There was no material reason why the United States should have been interested in a war in Manchuria except this:

The United States had taken the initiative in negotiating a treaty for the outlawry of war. The last nation had ratified the pact, and President Hoover had invited its author, Frank B. Kellogg, and all the diplomatic representatives of the nations which had signed it, to attend a gala ceremony at the White House, formally declaring the Pact in effect and war outlawed throughout the world.

And just on the eve of this ceremony, Russian and Chinese troops mobilized on the Manchu-Siberian frontier.

Mr. Stimson had the alternative of acting vigorously or seeing the Kellogg Pact and the White House ceremony become the laughing stock of the world. He was not, however, goaded into action by ridicule alone. Essentially slow-moving and lazy, ridicule supplied the kick-off, but when Henry Lewis Stimson got going, he went all the way. He made it clear that his action in throwing the entire weight of the United States against war was a precedent, and that thereafter the United States intended to set itself up as the protector of the Pact of Paris and the guardian of the peace of the world.

The brilliant audacity of Stimson's move left the Senate a little breathless. Few Senators will attack a man who is both belligerent and successful, and even those who had howled the loudest at Woodrow Wilson's entangling alliances now sat silent and approved. They did, that is, until Litvinoff slapped Stimson in the face. Then like all small boys who love a fight, they guffawed.

Litvinoff's slap could have been avoided. In the first place Stimson's battle had been pretty well won before Litvinoff retaliated. In the second place, although few people knew it, Stimson had been fighting on Litvinoff's side.

All during the controversy Mr. Stimson had championed the Russian cause. The chief bone of contention was whether China should return the Chinese Eastern Railroad before the dispute was arbitrated. Russia contended that the railroad had been seized illegally and that its future ownership could not be arbitrated fairly while it remained in the possession of China. Stimson backed Russia in this contention and he backed her to the limit. He summoned the meek little Chinese Minister, C. C. Wu, to his office, pounded on the desk and demanded that the railroad be turned back to Russia. His eyes snapped and his words rasped. When Stimson starts one of his pounding scenes he can be an awesome individual.

But after going to bat for Russia in a big way, Mr. Stimson, true to the habits he had formed as a rich man's son, went off to his Long Island estate for a Thanksgiving week-end.

When he left, Russian troops, having waited to take advantage of frozen ground, had advanced some eighty miles into Chinese territory. Mr. Stimson was absent for five days. During those five days the Russians completely evacuated Chinese soil. Mr. Stimson, when he returned, did not bother to read the telegrams the State Department had received reporting this evacuation and sent two sharply worded notes drawn up during his vacation, to China and Russia.

Litvinoff was in a position to reply that no Russian troops were on Chinese soil, and, with all the genius a Russian has for sarcasm and invective, he made the most of his opportunity.

Mr. Stimson probably regrets the time element in regard to his last note, but he has never regretted the stand he took to uphold the Kellogg Pact. Nor has he nursed any particular grudge against Litvinoff for the way he clouded an issue which otherwise would have stood out as the most courageous work Mr. Stimson performed during the first two years of his tumultuous State Department administration.

*

Mr. Stimson has confided to his friends that his greatest ambition before he became Secretary of State was to end the back-biting rivalry between Great Britain and the United States which reached its climax after the abortive Geneva Naval Conference, when France and Britain negotiated a secret agreement of their own and Mr. Coolidge, in retaliation, instructed Frank B. Kellogg to snub the British by sailing only within nose-thumbing distance of their shores while en route to Ireland in the summer of 1928. Mr. Stimson's hope was to negotiate, as the foundation for a new Anglo-American friendship, a new naval treaty.

Sincere as this ambition was, Mr. Stimson, as in most things, was pushed into it. Even before he became Secretary of State and was *en route* from the Philippines to Washington, the Japanese, worried about increased cruiser construction, got Stimson ashore at Tokyo, wined and dined him and emphasized the importance of holding a naval conference as soon as possible.

A day or two after his arrival in Washington, Stimson was called into a conference between President Hoover and Hugh Gibson, perpetual plenipotentiary for the United States at all disarmament conferences. These two had been planning some surprises for the French and British at the session of the Preparatory Commission on Disarmament opening in Geneva two weeks hence, and Stimson's capacity at that first conference was merely to listen and nod approval.

During all of those early naval negotiations through the summer of 1929, it was Hoover who did the pushing and

ambition had been to put an end to naval competition and to begin a new era of Anglo-American friendship. All eyes were on him.

And he muffed the ball.

His chief fault lay in the fact that he knew this was his supreme moment. He knew that all eyes were on him. He knew that responsibility for success or failure rested entirely on his shoulders. So he accepted every infinitesimal and unimportant responsibility there was to accept. He delegated little to others. He was surrounded by six American delegates, all touted by the Hoover Administration as headliners. Of these, four at least, deserved their reputations. Ambassador Dawes had been able to make a recalcitrant Europe accept a revision of reparations. Dwight W. Morrow had come out on top of a score of difficult negotiations in the Allied shipping controversy, to say nothing of the collapse of Cuba and the oil and religious controversies in Mexico. Senators Reed and Robinson were tried and trusted warriors who had been able to wheedle and jockey agreements out of difficult political alignments.

A good executive would have used these men. Stimson did not. To Reed and Morrow he delegated certain negotiations with the Japanese and the French. The other negotiations he kept chiefly in his own hands. And he worried over them. He fretted with detail. He became nervous and confused, until, sometimes at meetings of all seven delegates, six would be in unanimous agreement and an extra hour was necessary to bring the chief delegate—Mr. Stimson—into line.

Four factors contributed to Stimson's downfall at London:

Poor executive ability; the fact that at the State Department and during most of his life he has been surrounded with "yes" men, whereas at London he was surrounded by equals;

A slow-moving mind accustomed to taking days and even weeks to thresh out decisions;

The habit of relying on the whip hand he held in the

War Department, in Nicaragua and in the Philippines, and which was lacking in London;

Nervous fatigue.

The latter contributed to the delays and difficulties of the London Naval Conference more than any one outside the intimate circle of the American delegation has ever known.

There appears to be a lack of resilience in Stimson's physique, a lack of hardening to long hours of worrisome wear and tear. Perhaps this is the secret behind the long week-ends of exercise which he has insisted upon all his life. Or perhaps, on the other hand, the fact that he has always had this exercise proves to be his undoing when he is without it.

Stimson suffers from only one physical complaint. On a big-game hunting trip as a young man, a rifle back-fired and a piece of steel penetrated one eye. At times since then he has feared that he might lose the sight of that eye.

Whether this or something else was responsible, Stimson was perpetually worn out in London; and despite the fact that the fall of the French Cabinet gave him three weeks' breathing spell, despite the fact that he had two weeks on the high seas coming from and going to London, he took two months' rest in the Adirondacks immediately the treaty was ratified.

Probably the secret of his fatigue was the fact that Stimson was a country squire transplanted from his broad acres at Woodley and Highold, set down in a cramped London hotel and given the job of running a naval conference. After half a day of strenuous negotiations, Stimson was fagged out and literally gasped for a breath of his moors.

Knowing his own weakness for the wide open spaces, Stimson fortunately had provided himself with a country estate just outside of London, and in it he took refuge when the prospects of agreement looked blackest. So all the American delegation blessed Stanmore and there were those who said that without it no treaty would have been signed at all.

Next to his fatigue, which he could not prevent and which

therefore might be termed an act of God, no man-conceived problem so bedeviled Mr. Stimson as the now famous "consultative pact." This was largely Mr. Stimson's own fault. He arrived in London with a bland and vague idea in the back of his head that sometime when he got round to it he would have to give a little attention to some form of political concession to Europe.

And as with a great many other things which have mattered much in his life, he was rushed into a situation before he knew what it was all about.

The day the French delegation arrived in London forty-eight hours before the Conference had convened, Tardieu issued a diplomatic warning through the press that in return for a naval agreement he expected the United States to agree to consult with Europe in case war threatened in the Mediterranean. A few days later, when the Baltimore *Sun* and the New York *World* followed an account of a luncheon between Morrow, Reed, Briand and Tardieu with a report that the American delegation favored a consultative pact, Mr. Stimson authorized a vehement denial. During the next two weeks, the American delegation did nothing about a political concession to Europe and let a score of American journalists speculate daily as to whether the United States would or would not agree to consult with Europe in case of war.

Finally, when Secretary Stimson, at a journalistic luncheon, let drop the fact that he favored a consultative pact, American public opinion had been so see-sawed back and forth, so juggled up and down, for and against a consultative pact, that ratification in the Senate appeared unlikely and President Hoover finally cabled Stimson to drop it.

An impasse followed. It became clear that France was not going to sign the treaty unless she got some political concession from the United States, some pledge that the United States would not use her greatly augmented navy to break up any concerted boycott which the League of Nations might impose against an aggressor nation. That is, this became clear to almost every one except Mr. Stimson. Finally, Mr. Morrow undertook to bring his chief around to this point of view.

On Saturday, March 22, he hied himself to Stanmore, where he spent the day trying to persuade Mr. Stimson that the consultative pact was the key to the entire treaty situation; that if the United States would agree to consult, Great Britain would agree to the French naval figures, and France in turn would make concessions to Italy. Finally Mr. Morrow succeeded. Mr. Stimson told him he could go back to London and notify the other members of the American delegation.

Having done this, Mr. Morrow waited for Mr. Stimson to send a cable notifying the White House of the new move. Most of Sunday passed and no cable was sent. Finally Mr. Morrow motored back to Stanmore, trailed Mr. Stimson around the golf course, finally caught up with him and got him to send a cable to the President. The cable, however, was vague and poorly phrased. It failed to set forth the reasons which prompted Mr. Stimson to make his extraordinary move.

The next day, Monday, Mr. Morrow drafted his own cable, got Mr. Stimson's signature and sent it to the President.

But it was too late. Mr. Hoover, irritated by press reports that the consultative pact had been revived, and unconvinced by Stimson's first explanatory wire, issued a statement to the press condemning the consultative pact. Simultaneously Mr. Stimson in London was issuing a statement to the press explaining the terms on which the United States would accept a consultative pact.

The difference between those two gentlemen on this subject has never been reconciled.

\*

ELIHU ROOT is fond of telling a story on his young protégé, Henry Lewis Stimson, when the latter, then District Attorney for Southern New York, was riding one of his favorite horses in Rock Creek Park and met Theodore Roosevelt, then President, accompanied by Mr. Root, then Secretary of War. The creek was between them. Roosevelt, who knew Stimson, but did not recognize him at a distance, asked Root who the soldierly-looking horseman was.

"Lieutenant Stimson, of the New York National Guard," replied Root. And then, calling across the creek, he ordered:

"Lieutenant Stimson! The Secretary of War orders you to report to your Commander-in-Chief."

Stimson turned his horse and spurred him into the creek. The water was flooded and the horse at times went over his head. Stimson rode up the bank on the other side, reined in his mount and saluted.

The incident is illustrative of one of the most important points in Stimson's make-up. He is a fighter, but first of all he is a soldier. He obeys orders. He has courage, both moral and physical. He has guts and he has nerve. He will not retreat—except under one condition—if ordered.

As Secretary of State he has now got to the point where he encourages in his subordinates a great deal of discussion. He is liberal to the extent of listening to their views and usually accepting them. On occasion he gives orders. And when he gives them, he expects them to be obeyed.

There is only one man from whom Mr. Stimson, himself, takes orders. When he receives them, being a good soldier, he obeys.

Therefore when the President of the United States tells Mr. Stimson he is opposed to a consultative pact, when he tells him that he will not under any circumstances recognize Russia, when he tells him that he is opposed to too much American participation in the General Disarmament Conference at Geneva, Mr. Stimson obeys.

Mr. Stimson now has more definitely than ever made up his mind in favor of a consultative pact. He believes the Kellogg Treaty should be strengthened by providing some machinery to check war when it threatens. But the President is opposed to this; and Mr. Stimson, the good soldier, does not argue.

Mr. Stimson is sympathetically inclined toward Soviet Russia. Mr. Hoover has lost money in Russia, has had unfortunate food-relief experiences with Russia, is unalterably opposed to having the remotest possible contact with Russia. Mr. Stimson does not argue.

Mr. Stimson believes that a serious situation confronts Europe. He believes that unless Europe can show some really tangible reduction of armament, the seeds of another war are as good as sprouted. Mr. Hoover points out that too much American participation in European affairs will react against his reëlection in 1932. Mr. Stimson, always the good soldier, obeys orders.

Henry Lewis Stimson has come to be a much more effective and efficient Secretary of State. His memory is still bad but he controls his temper. He has surrounded himself, on the whole, with good men. He has won their loyalty. Most difficult of all, he now gets along even with the newspapermen and the Senate.

Mr. Stimson is a home-loving man. One of the tragedies in his life is the fact that he has no children. He has surrounded himself with pets and has all but adopted Captain Eugene Regnier, his military aide, not because he needs an aide, but because down deep in his heart he needs a son. Regnier, naïve, charming and with a streak of fundamental good sense, comes nearer being that than he does anything else.

So Mr. Stimson, always the country squire, each day lives in anticipation of the early afternoon when he can leave the routine of the State Department and go out to see his dogs and his parrot and wander over his expansive acres at Woodley.

There, before an open fireplace in the late afternoon or early morning, Mr. Stimson is at peace with the world.

ments, especially the army and navy, is taken into consideration. However, despite the fact that the State Department is no worse than any of the others, its reputation is just the opposite. In Washington it is called the most inefficient, dilatory, procrastinating and red-tape-bound bureaucracy in the government service. Outside of Washington, businessmen compare it unfavorably with the Department of Commerce, while editors leap at opportunities to pooh-pooh the slightest tendency toward white-spats and namby-pambyism on the part of its officers.

The State Department has played all the trump cards in its hand in order to live down this reputation. The Secretary of State has made speeches, the Under-Secretary has gone on a barn-storming trip, and the Bureau of Current Information has inspired articles—all to no avail. The fact remains that most people in the United States, who have ever heard of the State Department at all, have heard of it as a social club whose members are selected from blue-stocking Bostonians, wield their forks with their left hands, and are no more representative of American life than the Redskins whom their ancestors pushed west.

Broadly speaking, this is not true. There is just enough truth in it, however, to make the picture persist. Out of the four thousand-odd diplomats, consuls, clerks, and stenographers, who represent the State Department both at home and abroad, only a few hundred honestly deserve the epithets they get. However, these few not only are completely impossible, but also happen to be placed in strategic places where they constantly and consistently act as a cinder in the public eye.

There are two other concrete reasons why the State Department's unenviable reputation continues to persist.

First, there is a sense of self-importance inspired by association with monarchs and their ambassadors which turns the heads of almost every young man, even though he comes from Kalamazoo or Keokuk and arrives for his first State

Department examination with the back of his neck shaved and a nasal twang that sends cold shivers down the spine of the chief officer of protocol.

Second, the career men of the State Department were given their chance in 1925, failed to grasp it, and have never been able to live down that failure.

How great their opportunity and how disastrous their failure, few people who did not witness it realize.

*

AFTER years of effort to take the Diplomatic and Consular Services out of politics, the career men in 1924 succeeded in pushing the Rogers Act through Congress. This amalgamated the two services on the same salary basis, boosted pay all around, provided that all career men begin at the bottom of the ladder and climb up, gave them the opportunity to become Ministers and Ambassadors and, in general, took the foreign service out of politics.

The Rogers Act also drew a sharp caste line between the foreign service, or career men, on the one hand, and the drafting officers on the other. Drafting officers are permanently appointed to serve in the State Department and never go abroad to serve in legations and embassies. Men of more brains than means, they frequently write the orders which the Ambassador in the field must carry out. The career, or foreign service, officers, on the other hand, are supposed to spend practically all of their time abroad, being allowed to come back to Washington occasionally for short periods of service in the State Department. Their salaries are higher than those of the drafting officers, and they also receive small allowances for rent, teas, dinners, receptions, wreaths, birthday gifts and other means by which a diplomat justifies his retention in a foreign capital.

Within the foreign service itself, the Rogers Act failed to eradicate a second caste line, not so sharply drawn, however, between the consuls and the diplomats. In theory, the two branches of the service are one, and a man may transfer back and forth between them. Actually, however, the diplomats look down upon the consuls, who have to keep regular office hours and bother with such plebeian routine as bills of lading, clearance papers, reporting trade opportunities and sending home the clothes of dead seamen. The diplomatic branch requires money, a broad Bostonian A, and the knack of handling a tea-cup. There are about one hundred career diplomats and over four hundred career consuls in the service.

The Rogers Act put this diplomatic group of career men on top of the State Department. They could get anything they wanted and their appetites were insatiable. Frank B. Kellogg, nervous, inexperienced, had just come back from the Court of St. James. Qualified to become Secretary of State only because he was one of the very few Senators who had chatted occasionally with Calvin Coolidge, then a very much snubbed Vice President, Kellogg relied on the career men.

He found as his Under-Secretary, Joseph Clark Grew, wealthy descendant of the Boston Cabots, and related by marriage to the House of Morgan. Not knowing what else to do with his time or his money, Grew decided that the Diplomatic Service was as pleasant and patriotic a career as any and had prepared for it by tiger shooting in Manchuria, elephant hunting in India, and a clerkship in the American consulate in Cairo at the age of twenty-four. In the twenty years which followed, he had made an excellent record for himself and attained the rank of Minister. As Under-Secretary of State, however, Grew was in constant hot water. The administration of a legation abroad with a staff of three or four, he discovered, was far different from the problem of running a high-powered machine employing six hundred people which grinds out American foreign policy for every part of the world.

With Grew, in the inner sanctuary of the State Department, were J. Butler Wright, arbiter of protocol and diplomatic dress; Leland Harrison, scion of a wealthy New York family; and Hugh Robert Wilson, heir of the Chicago shirt manufacturer. These men ran the State Department. They appointed themselves and their own tried and trusted friends as members of the Personnel Board to pass upon promotions. They picked their friends for the best foreign posts and saw to it that the amenable Mr. Kellogg got them approved at the White House. Every time such an appointment came back from the White House bearing the initials "C. C.," Hugh Wilson, in charge of press relations, called in the newspapermen and whispered "most confidentially" that a certain appointment was about to be announced, that it was to be a great triumph for the principle of a career service and that the newspapers would do well to play it up as such.

The career diplomats had the wheel and they drove the Department at a to-hell-with-every-one-else clip straight down their own narrow road.

That road led to the famous State Department smash of 1927. During that smash everything that possibly could break against the controlling career clique did break. The Senate Foreign Relations Committee launched an investigation of the career service. Mrs. Edith Nourse Rogers, widow of the author of the Rogers Act, introduced a bill aimed to patch up the holes which the clique was taking advantage of. Senator Moses succeeded in getting a similar bill passed by the Senate. The late Representative Steve Porter, Chairman of the House Foreign Affairs Committee, introduced a bill calculated to do the same thing. Representative Edwards of Georgia introduced a resolution exposing the fact that the wealthier and more favored diplomats had been promoted at a far faster rate than the less wealthy and less favored consuls. Lawrence Dennis, Chargé d'Affaires of the American Legation in Nicaragua, resigned after writing a scathing rebuke of the favoritism displayed by the career clique. Tracy Lay, American Consul General at Buenos Aires and one of the authors of the Rogers Act, followed him. John Gray, Secretary at the American Legation in Panama, did the same. Every newspaper in the country carried articles and editorials denouncing the self-promotion plan of the career men. And worst of all, big business, the god whom the State Department strives chiefly to serve, joined in the denunciation. Victor M. Cutter, President of the United Fruit Company and who ought to know diplomats, made a speech before the high moguls of big business gathered at the annual meeting of the United States Chamber of Commerce, denouncing the career men as lounge lizards and displayers of the white spat; while *The Magazine of Wall Street* published a scathing article, illustrated with sketches of a high hat, stick, gloves, spats and all the accouterments of the career service.

As result of all this, the career clique's bubble burst with tremendous reverberations and the following consequences:

1. The ring-leaders of the inner circle, Joe Grew, J. Butler Wright, Leland Harrison, Hugh Wilson, having seen the hand-writing on the wall, appointed themselves as Ambassador to Turkey, Minister to Hungary, Minister to Sweden and Minister to Switzerland, respectively, just before the smash occurred.

2. Frank B. Kellogg was forced to come out with an acknowledgment that Representative Edwards' criticism of favoritism toward diplomats as against consuls was valid, and he, Kellogg, proceeded to correct the injustice by promoting a long list of consuls.

3. Henry L. Stimson entered the office of Secretary of State one year and a half later, nursing a profound distrust of career diplomats.

The career scandals of 1927-28 have not yet been lived down. Nor will they be. The glaring favoritism and high-handed snobbery practised by the clique in those days is no more, but enough of it still exists to make the State Department, and especially the career service, a most vulnerable target.

The men who steered the service in the old days of its rampant glory have been dispersed but are still functioning.

Their creed is snobbery, favoritism, self-protection, ultra-conservatism, and assiduity in pleasing the Secretary of State.

Illustrative of their frame of mind is Robert Wood Bliss, now exiled to Argentina as American Ambassador and a high priest of the career men. His training in exclusiveness began at an early age when his father, manager of the firm which manufactures "Castoria—Children Cry For It," took as his second wife, Mrs. Anna Blakeley Barnes, owner of the firm. Young Bliss then married his step-mother's daughter, Mildred. The marriage has been a most happy one and has the added advantage of keeping in the family the tremendous fortune rolled up by "Castoria," a product which Washington children cry for in vain because Ambassador Bliss's desire to live down his plebeian ancestry has caused him to rule that his father's and step-mother's medicine shall not be advertised in the District of Columbia.

Herbert Hoover, after watching Bliss work at Buenos Aires during the Presidential good-will trip, decided to appoint a new Ambassador to Argentina, but came home to find that Bliss had been a heavy contributor to the Republican campaign fund. In order to take no chances, Bliss usually contributed to the campaign funds of both parties. His rise has been rapid.

Before Bliss became an Ambassador, however, and while he was merely an Assistant Secretary of State, he once pulled a *pièce de résistance* of snobbery which used to be typical of the career clique and which still is typical of their mental attitude. Bliss was giving two receptions for the State Department at his beautiful Georgetown mansion, inhabited only by a caretaker seven-eighths of the time, and had invited to the first reception all of the members of the career service. To the second reception, he had invited the clerks, stenographers and lesser lights, together with the drafting officers, many of whom outranked the career men.

Harry Dwight, Chief of the Near Eastern Division, author of "Stamboul Nights," a high-ranking person but a drafting officer, had received an invitation to the first reception for the career service. Discovering this fact, Bliss recalled the invitation and asked Dwight to come to the second reception for the common people.

There was nothing unusual about Bliss's social snobbery. It is rather common in the State Department. The social line drawn between the foreign service officer of the select career service and the drafting officer who sometimes rises from a clerkship used to be as strict as the distinction between Brahmin and untouchable. To some it still is. Joshua Butler Wright is of the old school. He does not appear to be. He once punched cattle on a Wyoming ranch and still labors under the delusion that he can mix with "folks." His old job as Assistant Secretary of State did not give him much time for this, however. He was the State Department's glad-hander and took pride in his work. Every ticket-puncher and porter at the Union Station knew him. There was even a rumor that some of them called him "Butsy." The sight of Joshua Butler Wright, attired in Bond Street topper, cutaway, tailored in Saville Row, cream-colored gloves and malacca stick, strolling down to Gate Number 18 was the cue to every employee in the Union Station that a new Ambassador was arriving in town.

Despite the fact, however, that Butsy may have been "Butsy" to the hired help at the Union Station, he took his social P's and Q's just as seriously as does Dolly Curtis Gann; so that on one occasion when the German Embassy was giving a dinner and Prentiss Gilbert, then a mere drafting officer, was invited, Assistant Secretary of State Wright informed Mr. Gilbert that there must have been some mistake.

Those were the halcyon days when the State Department was a rich man's club and no one was afraid to admit it. Its members took this for granted. In fact, many of them opposed the Rogers Bill boosting salaries because they sincerely believed that high salaries would open the gates of diplomacy to *hoi polloi* and that the responsibility for representing the U.S.A. abroad should fall only on the shoulders of the wealthy few.

No one is very brazen about admitting such a thing these days, but, occasionally, in shadowy corners of the Metropolitan Club one hears whispers that the career service is not what it was in the good old days when a substantial private fortune was necessary in order to become a Third Secretary of Legation.

As a matter of fact, it still takes nothing short of a miracle for a man to get transferred from the consular to the diplomatic branch of the service unless he has a private income, at least a small one. This is one of the factors which tends to make the career service so unpopular with the general public.

The general public, traveling in Europe for the first time in the person of a school teacher from Wichita or a banker from Pueblo, drops in at the American Embassy in Paris or Madrid with the feeling that he is helping to pay for the up-keep of the place and might possibly run across some of the folks from home. However, he meets there a young man with glasses who has spent all of his life since graduation in the rarefied atmosphere of pink teas, protocol and diplomacy, who knows nothing of the United States outside of Cambridge, New York, Bar Harbor and Washington, who has soiled his hands at no manual labor more arduous than bridge, and the result is a clash which not only does not enhance the prestige of the foreign service back in Kansas and Colorado but which makes the young man feel that his country is populated with hicks who don't deserve to have their interests protected.

The result of all this is that the career service has never been known to sympathize with any point of view other than that of entrenched wealth. Its members are ideally qualified to protect the interests of those who contribute to the Coolidge and Hoover Administrations. Most of them have spent their lives hanging on to what their fathers made. The business man who has made money on his own initiative is rare in their midst, and as a result, their approach to every problem is negative rather than positive. Their motto is that which hangs in Pull-